M000274905

Ronald Johnson

Magic Happens!

MY JOURNEY WITH THE
NORTHERN IOWA WIND SYMPHONY

Maxime's Music

Copyright © 2020 Ronald Johnson

PUBLISHED BY MAXIME'S MUSIC

CONCERTBANDMUSICSTORE.COM

All rights reserved. This book or any portion thereof may not be reproduced or used in any manner whatsoever without the express written permission of the publisher except for the use of brief quotations in a book review.

Printed in the United States of America

First printing, November 2020

ISBN: 978-1-936512-90-4

Contents

List of Figures

6

List of Tables

Preface

THIS IS A STORY ABOUT MAGIC ... a story about love, and inspiration, and discovery. It is also the story of a journey ... my journey. And, as with most journeys, the path from before to now was not a straight one ... it was not without missteps, errors, slips, blunders, and disappointments. This is an account of my 35-year journey with the wonderful students of the University of Northern Iowa Wind Symphony. It is a story of what we did together in those 35 years ... of where we started, where we traveled and, eventually, where we ended. It is a story of what we accomplished together ... what we hoped for, what we dreamed, what we created. Our story is not intended as prescriptive ... a model for others to follow or imitate. It, simply, is our story.

Ronald Johnson, September 2020
Cedar Falls, Iowa

Acknowledgements

FROM THE TIME I WAS SIX YEARS OLD, each year, in late August
or early September, I started to school . . . either as a student or as
a teacher. Throughout my life, I was surrounded by teachers and
other mentors who cared for me, inspired me, encouraged me, and
loved me. Many of those people are included in this story, but, for
purposes of the story line, many are not. Still, I am a product of all
those who have shared my journey with me, and allowed me to be
part of theirs. Indeed, I could not have had the life I did without
them. With them, I found . . . and, am still finding . . . who I am
now, who I could become, and what I intend to represent.

When I was in the 8th grade, I discovered the world of music,
by means of percussion. In this world, I found the composers,
conductors, and performers who would inspire me and motivate
me for the remainder of my life. In this world, I found the power of
great music to inspire us . . . to touch our hearts, to heal our souls,
to help us become whole human beings. From that moment in the
8th grade until now, I have lived my life in two worlds . . . the world
of music, and the world of teaching.

There are several people who encouraged me, and helped me with
the writing of this book. Each of them was needed for this story
to become reality. The first of these is Caroline Francis, Communications and Operations Coordinator in the School of Music at
the University of Northern Iowa, and my good friend. In our many
lunch conversations, when I would recount stories of events from

our European tours or the impetus for one of our past projects, Caroline would often say, "You have to write this down! This is such a great story!" It was she who asked about the origins of ideas, projects, and other elements of our development. She was helpful as a reader of the text … questioning this, suggesting that, encouraging me to reveal more of what we did. I also give thanks to Lawrence Harper, Emeritus Director of Bands at Carroll University in Wisconsin. Larry has been a close friend and colleague for almost fifty years now, and has enjoyed a distinguished career as conductor and teacher. Larry read the text several times, offering suggestions (most of which I took), and finding small, almost hidden, errors of spelling or syntax. And, enormous thanks to Melody Steed, Professional Organist and Elementary Music Teacher, and long-time friend. Melody was relentless in her attempts to bring clarity and "readability" to the narrative. She read the complete text several times, and each time found new questions for me … questions which were always helpful and productive.

Finally, I am thankful to the hundreds of marvelous students with whom I was privileged to work, and make music, for all those many years. While I became a year older each fall, they were always the same age … they always came with hopes and dreams for a better tomorrow, and a willingness to invest in their lives. Every year, they brought me new things to think about … different ways of doing things, questions that I had not considered before. They inspired me with their spiritual courage to continue their journey when conditions of their lives often made that quite difficult. It was from them that I learned that no one goes unscathed in this life … that we all carry a burden, and that we all have wounds, no matter how we may try to hide them. To find healing for our Souls in the spiritual realm of great music … that was always their gift to me. I think of them every day now, and I am grateful.

Introduction

WHEN I WAS AN UNDERGRADUATE student at Texas Tech University (at that time, Texas Technological College), if someone had suggested to me that I would spend thirty-five years of my life at the University of Northern Iowa (UNI) doing what I got to do, I would not have believed it. Not only was my level of preparation insufficient for what would come later, but the very notion that such a life was available was not in my realm of possibilities. Simply put, I had no idea that this world even existed.

My dream as an undergraduate was to be a high school band director. In Texas, in the late 1960s, high school band directors held positions of influence equal to that of administrators and athletic coaches. Interestingly, it was the one of the few goals that I was never able to achieve. After graduation in the spring of 1968, I spent one year teaching and conducting the band at Robert T. Hill Junior High in Dallas, Texas. I loved the job, and the kids. We won contests and received awards. But, sometime around mid-year, I realized that I was relying on the excellent preparation supplied by my predecessor and that, in the next year, I would have to face my own teaching. So, I determined to leave Dallas, and move to California and pursue a Master's degree, and career, in percussion.

My percussion teacher at Tech, Joel Leach, had taken a position at San Fernando Valley State College (SFVSC), later renamed California State University, Northridge (CSUN). So, I followed him there in the fall semester of 1969. Joel had an enormous influence

"And I would answer you . . . that to prepare the future is only to found the present . . . for the sole true invention is to decipher the present under its incoherent aspects and its contradictory language . . . You do not have to foresee the future, but to allow it."
~ Antoine de Saint-Exupéry ~

on me as an undergraduate, and it was he to whom I looked for advice and counsel in finding my direction. My hope was to become an orchestral and/or studio player in Los Angeles. I was fairly capable as a percussionist and had no other real burning desires as a musician. The idea of conducting had not shown up yet. Indeed, I had no idea of what being a conductor meant. I knew "band directing," but that was a long way from the world I was about to enter.

Coincidentally, though I have since come to understand that nothing happens by chance, that was also the first year for David Whitwell, as Conductor of the Wind Ensemble. The Chairman of the Music Department, Clarence Wiggins, had been the conductor since the university opened in 1958. But, the university was growing rapidly, requiring that he give more of his energy to administrative duties. So, in the summer of 1969, he hired Dr. Whitwell, who had just returned from Vienna, where he had spent the previous year working for the Austrian music publisher, Universal Edition; doing wind history research in several major libraries, and conducting concerts and recording sessions with several major European symphony orchestras. The arrival of David Whitwell was to change my direction . . . and my life . . . forever.

Figure 1: David Whitwell

That fall, I was assigned to the Wind Ensemble as a member of the percussion section. I can still remember that first rehearsal ... Dr. Whitwell entering the rehearsal room; welcoming the students; calling for a tuning note, and beginning to rehearse Hector Berlioz' *Grande Symphonie Funebre et Triomphale.* There was no score in front of him; no music stand. He had memorized the score, as was his practice for the entirety of his career. It was amazing. I had never heard music like this before. My undergraduate experience had been marches, orchestral transcriptions, some novelty tunes, and works from the standard repertoire which were known as "war horses." I remember leaving that first rehearsal and going out to sit in the courtyard and recover from the experience. I was in emotional distress from the power of this exquisite music. The rehearsals following were equally fulfilling, and the concerts that fall were exhilarating.

For the spring semester, I asked Dr. Whitwell if I could study with him privately, now realizing that, perhaps, conducting was my true calling. We spent the semester with him teaching me the basics of score study, and introducing me to the world of Art Music ... again, something of which I knew nothing. We listened to, and studied Strauss, and Mahler, and Wagner, and a host of other celebrated composers. It was in this time that I began to understand that it was the composer and the music which was important, that the ensemble was only the messenger, not the message. My previous experience was that attention was given to the ensemble (the band), and less attention to what music was performed. So, this notion of the primacy of the composer, and the importance of the aesthetic quality of the composition ... these were new ideas for me. The following year, I continued to study with him, but now as Assistant Conductor of the Wind Orchestra. Dr. Whitwell had changed the name in the previous spring semester. He allowed me to rehearse every week, and conduct on every concert. What a wonderful gift that was for me!

In the spring semester of 1971, on a Friday in May, the Wind Orchestra was scheduled for an evening "run-out" concert at Santa Barbara High School, one of the better music programs in the southern

"A life without once reading Hamlet is like a life spent in a coal mine."
~ Hector Berlioz ~

part of the state. The group was loaded on to the bus, waiting in the front parking lot of the music building, and ready to leave. Almost at the moment the bus started to move, the department secretary came running out of the building, frantically waving her arms. (*This, of course, was a time before cell phones and computers. Once the bus left, it would have been several hours before contact would have been possible.*) The secretary told Dr. Whitwell that his wife was at the hospital; she was in labor, and their first child was about to be born. As I remember the moment, he calmly handed me the scores for the concert, indicated that he would try and join us at a later time, and bade me farewell. While I had been present for all rehearsals, I had not conducted any rehearsals on my own, except for the piece I was to conduct. The program included H. Owen Reed's *La Fiesta Mexicana*, Jacques Ibert's *Concerto for Cello and Wind Instruments*, Henk Badings' *Armageddon*, and a couple of other first rate pieces—none of which I had ever conducted.

I asked the principal players to come to the front of the bus and talk to me about tempi, and what happened at certain structural points in the music. I had about two hours, as I remember, before the concert. Somehow, we made it through the program without major problems. Dr. Whitwell never made it out of the hospital. I am certain that the performance was not all that wonderful—it couldn't have been! But, those were good players, who were well prepared and they helped me along. For me, of course, it was a pivotal moment in my life. While I am sure that I was quite scared of what was happening in the moment, it was also thrilling to stand in front of the ensemble, allowing the sounds of that remarkable music to wash over my body and soul. I was hooked—there was no turning back now. I was now on my path.

The following fall (1971), I joined the faculty on a part-time basis, working with the marching band, teaching a jazz history course, and continuing my work as Assistant Conductor of the Wind Orchestra. In the spring (1972), with the help and support of Dr. Wiggins, department chair, I was able to take a sabbatical replacement position for the band director at Bakersfield College, a two-year (junior) college, about one hundred miles north of the San Fernando

"Maybe, the journey isn't so much about becoming anything. Maybe, it's about unbecoming everything that isn't really you, so you can be who you were meant to be in the first place."
~ Anonymous ~

Valley. Wiggins had been department chair there before his tenure at SFVSC, and had good connections with the administration. There was a pretty good band program there, though more well known for its jazz band. I no longer have concert programs from that time in Bakersfield, but do remember performing the *Requiem for Louis XVI* by Nicolas-Charles Bochsa (France, 1789–1856), and Henk Badings' (Netherlands, 1907–1987) *Armageddon*.

That summer, I was hired to teach percussion at the Idyllwild School of Music and the Arts (ISOMATA), a summer program sponsored by the University of Southern California (USC). As I remember, I was there for about four weeks. The program was quite famous, with many nationally and internationally acclaimed musicians having been "campers" there, when younger. My duties were to rehearse the percussion sections for the wind ensemble and orchestra, and to teach private lessons in percussion. I also conducted the wind ensemble for one week (there were several conductors that summer) and directed the jazz band for a couple of weeks.

As the summer was coming to a close, I was beginning to seriously consider what I might do in the fall, as I had no prospects. I had applied for several small college positions, but had not received any response. By the beginning of August, I was beginning to lose hope. I had pretty much resigned myself to living with my mother, and playing dance gigs and whatever other part-time work I could find in the Los Angeles area. I decided to take what little money I had, and fly to Las Vegas for one last "party" before reality was to set in. I flew to Vegas on a Saturday, partied for the remainder of the day and night (I didn't even book a hotel room) and flew back the next day. I arrived late, maybe 9:00 PM or so, and drove from the airport in Pomona up the mountain to Idyllwild. It was a Sunday night, before the last week of the camp, at around 10:00 PM. Before heading to my room for sleep, I decided to stop by the mail room to see if I had any messages. There, in my mailbox, was a pink message slip with the written words, "Call Modesto Junior College," along with a name and number for me to call. I had applied for the Director of Bands job there earlier in the spring, but had heard nothing from them. I still have no idea how they knew where to find me. Things

"And every day, the world will drag you by the hand, yelling: 'This is important! And, this is important! You need to worry about this! And, this! And, this!' And, each day, it's up to you to yank your hand back, put it over your heart, and say: 'No. This is what's important.'"
~ Iain Thomas ~

were much different in the 1970s, and communications were limited to phones with land lines, and the US Postal Service. In any case, I called Modesto the next morning, and they invited me to fly up for an interview. A day or two later, I flew from Pomona to Modesto (this was before airline deregulation) did the interview, and they offered me the position!

Several years later, I learned that the President of Bakersfield College, Dr. Burns Finlinson, had phoned the President of Modesto College—apparently, they had been good friends—and had given me a glowing recommendation saying how successful was my one semester tenure there. I am forever grateful for his generous support and exceptional kindness.

Two weeks after the interview, I packed all my worldly possessions into a small trailer attached to the back of my car, and drove to Modesto to start my new life. Three weeks earlier, I had been at the lowest point of my life to that point, with no idea of what to do or where to go. Now, I was soaring with the eagles, my heart bursting with excitement and my soul filled with dreams of what might be possible in Modesto. I was 27-years-old—just a baby!

I was there for seven of the best years of my life.

MODESTO JUNIOR COLLEGE (MJC) was founded in 1921; one of more than one hundred two-year colleges in California. The enrollment in 1972 was around 15,000 students. At the time of my arrival, junior colleges in the state were essentially the first two years of a four-year degree program with students finishing their degrees at one of the thirty-three public universities in California. That would change later to a more "technical" curriculum: police training, nursing, landscape design, etc. The College enjoyed enormous popularity in the community, with around 90% of the population having some connection—taking a "night course," attending a performance on campus—something.[1] The campus was beautiful, and the auditorium was excellent, a WPA project from the 1940s.

[1] George Lucas is a graduate of MJC. His first successful film was *American Graffiti*, a story of his youth in Modesto. "American Graffiti Days" is still celebrated annually.

When I arrived in late August of 1972, I was young and ambitious . . .
eager to prove myself in the larger world of university bands and
wind ensembles. I changed the name of the group from "Symphonic
Band" to "Wind Symphony." My association with Dr. Whitwell
helped me to formulate opinions about the name one chooses for
their performing ensembles. I came to feel that the term, "band,"
gave the listener . . . especially Americans . . . the impression of a
repertoire that consisted primarily of lighter pieces, marches, and
orchestral transcriptions. That certainly was the type of music I
played in high school and college. The newer term, "wind ensemble," . . . created by Frederick Fennell at the Eastman School of
Music in 1952 . . . seemed to give the impression of a more serious
literature selection, but a smaller group; something closer to chamber music. Indeed, Maestro Fennell's initial repertoire selection
was 1/3 brass, 1/3 woodwinds, 1/3 percussion . . . mostly with single
players on a part.[2]

[2] The reader can find more specific information on Frederick Fennell and the Eastman
Wind Ensemble in other publications.

I felt that the term, "Wind Symphony," signaled a group of serious
intent, and also seemed to indicate a larger number of players.
"Wind Orchestra" was another term I seriously considered. It, too,
has grown in popularity . . . especially in European countries. Both
"Wind Symphony" and "Wind Orchestra" have equivalents in all
European languages . . . *blasorchester, symphonie á vénts, orchestra di
fiati*, and several others.

There were good students in those first few years. We became
popular in the community, and had large audiences for our concerts.
We instituted a practice of two performances for each concert
program . . . on Friday and Saturday nights. We drew 300–400
people each night. Later, we added a "campus" concert in the
Student Center on the Thursday of Concert Week, and . . . a little
later . . . a concert at a high school in the area on the following
Monday. This was the hey-day of American higher education, and
funding was excellent. I received funding for a week-long festival,
which I named the Festival of Winds. There were several events
each day . . . rehearsals, masterclasses, concerts, and other events.
We had a mix of professional artists and ensembles, university
groups from around the state, and our own student performers.

*"The simplest questions are the most profound.
Where were you born? Where is your home?
Where are you going? What are you doing? Think
about those once in a while, and watch your
answers change.*
~ Richard Bach ~

Among the professionals invited were Karel Husa (Pulitzer Prize, 1969); Toccatas and Flourishes (trumpet-organ duo featuring the Rodgers Touring Organ); the Eastern Brass Quintet; Blackearth Percussion Group; the Westwood Quintet; Cincinnati Early Music Group; the United States Air Force Band with Arnald Gabriel; and several others. We invited several of the finer university wind groups from the Los Angeles and San Francisco areas. This was a free event, sponsored by the College. It was enormously popular in the community, and was presented four or five years ... until passage of the infamous Proposition 13 in 1978.[3]

[3] For more on the impact of the introduction of Proposition 13, see page 30.

The Wind Symphony achieved a local, regional, and even somewhat national, reputation for excellent performances of serious wind literature. The group was invited to perform for the Western Division Conference of the College Band Directors National Association (CBDNA) in 1974; the CBDNA National Convention in 1975, and the National Wind Ensemble Conference in Los Angeles, also in 1975. At this time, I became quite active in professional organizations such as the CBDNA, MENC, and others. Because of my experiences with the Wind Symphony performing at both national and regional conferences, I began to form opinions about their value for the students and the institution. I discovered that travel costs for the group to perform at these events to be quite expensive ... buses, rental truck for percussion equipment, hotels, meals. In each of the occasions indicated above, the concert at the conference was the only one ... no other performances scheduled along the way. Because of the excellent performances by the students of a repertoire often unfamiliar to the audiences, these experiences helped to elevate my standing in the profession.

I was elected President of the CBDNA, Western Division, was a member of several national committees, and participated in several other professional gatherings of regional or national importance. Later, I came to understand that while our appearances at these conferences had helped to enhance my personal reputation in the profession, they had done little, if anything, for the reputation of the students or the institution. So, when I was invited to join the faculty at Northern Iowa, these experiences weighed on my mind—

and, my soul. I determined to find performance venues in which
the students ... the Wind Symphony ... were the focus; not myself.
I came to believe that the huge investment of time and money
should be of great benefit to the students, and the university. So,
with the exception of a few performances at the annual gathering
of the Iowa Bandmasters Association, we never performed at a
regional or national conference. Instead, we devoted our energies
to campus concerts, audio and video recordings, and European
concert tours.

IT WAS DURING my time in Modesto that I developed many of the
wonderful professional relationships that were to influence me
throughout my career. It was primarily through the CBDNA that I
was able to meet, and work with, several of the most outstanding
leaders in the profession. One of my early heroes was Frederick Fennell, famed conductor and founder of the Eastman Wind Ensemble
(EWE). I first became aware of Fred when I was a beginning "drummer" in the 8th grade at Matthews Junior High in Lubbock, Texas.
My band director, Morris Goolsby ... a great teacher and a great
influence ... gave me his vinyl LP of Fennell/Eastman's recording,
Ruffles and Flourishes. This was a recording, only released a couple of
years earlier, of military signals and calls for trumpets and drums,
and was the first recording I had ever heard of this kind of music.
It opened a new world for me, and was the impetus for my initial
thoughts about pursuing a life in music. When I got to college, I
found more recordings of Mr. Fennell and the EWE. Many college
and university bands were making recordings at this time, but they
were mostly from live performances, with repertoire consisting
primarily of marches, orchestral transcriptions, and perhaps some
novelty tunes. The Eastman recordings were quite different. Not
only was the repertoire dramatically different from most other
college band recordings of that era ... Hindemith, Schönberg,
Stravinsky, Milhaud, Gabrieli, and Mozart ... but the quality of the
recording process, and the skill of the players, was so much better.
These recordings became the standard by which all other college
wind groups would be measured, and they were an inspiration to

thousands, maybe hundreds of thousands, of young musicians and aspiring conductors.

Figure 2: Frederick Fennell

I first met Maestro Fennell at the Midwest Clinic in Chicago, in December of 1973 or 1974. I was introduced to him by my teacher and mentor, David Whitwell. David was always so helpful for me at conferences and conventions; shepherding me around … making sure that I met the best people in the profession; heard the best performances at the event, and looked at new scores and recordings. He always introduced me as a colleague, not as one of his students. His guidance in this period was more helpful for my growth and development than any other person or factor. After that first meeting with Fred, I kept in touch … I still have a whole file of handwritten letters from him. I collected copies of all the magazine articles that he wrote; mostly articles offering performance suggestions for many of the great masterpieces for wind groups … Holst, Grainger, Vaughan Williams, etc.

Around 1977, I invited him to come to Modesto to conduct the Wind Symphony in a performance of Gordon Jacob's *William Byrd Suite*. The work had long been a favorite of mine … I still consider it to be one of the most eloquent pieces in the repertoire … and, the Eastman recording was quite compelling. Fred was with us for several days, as I remember, and the experience was magical for both me and the students. He was such an expressive and "in the moment" conductor, and his whole persona was imbued with the mysterious workings of the music at hand. Of course, we had several meals together, and long talks after the concerts. He shared with me many stories of his childhood, growing up in Cleveland, Ohio, as well as many personal experiences that had an impact on his life. Later that year, I attended the 25th Anniversary of the founding of the Eastman Wind Ensemble in Rochester, New York. Again, I was able to spend several private moments with Fred, listening intently as he told me stories about his time as a student at Eastman, and the early years of his tenure there.

Some years later, during my doctoral studies at the University of Illinois, the composer, Francis McBeth, had been invited to campus for a workshop of some sort. I had known Francis from my days as a student at Texas Tech, when he often came for rehearsals or concerts. During his week in Illinois, we had lunch one day, and I told him about the topic for my doctoral dissertation, which was to be the history of the development of the wind ensemble movement in this country. The Eastman group was to be part of my study. Francis told me that he had just recently received a lengthy letter from Fred . . . some twenty-five single-spaced typewritten pages . . . telling of the formulation of the impetus for the founding of the wind ensemble, and for the ten years after that, before Fred left to become Associate Conductor for the Minnesota Orchestra. Francis was able to send me a copy of that letter . . . I contacted Fred to get his permission to use part of the story in my dissertation. A few years later, Fred published an expanded version of this letter under the title, *The Wind Ensemble.*

Frederick Fennell was a giant in our profession, occupying a place of honor reserved for few others. He was a hero and model for hundreds, maybe thousands, of young conductors from all over the planet. There are thousands of high school and college students who still remember that special moment when Fred Fennell was their guest conductor. For me, he was a mentor and friend. I had the week with him in Modesto in 1977, and the days during the 25th Anniversary celebration later that spring, plus several meetings at conferences and conventions. In fact, one of my photos of him during that anniversary event made its way into one of several books about his life.

When I was President of the CBDNA, Western Division, I helped fund a summer workshop at Saddleback College in southern California, with him as clinician. In the late 70s, Fred was about the only one doing conducting workshops. It didn't take long before others started to offer such events, but Fred was the original . . . he was the one who pointed the way for the rest of us. In 2015, someone made a video montage of his life.[4] In it, there is a small clip of that summer workshop in 1978 . . . maybe a minute or two. One can see the energy and creativity that Fred brought to every occasion.

Of course, there are numerous videos of Fred conducting; either in performance or in rehearsal. And, every one of them is a lesson in excellence. He always brought his "A game." He was one of a kind . . . there was no other like him. Without him, the profession would have never made it out of the Dark Ages . . . we would never have put forth the effort to realize our potential for artistic merit. We were different because he was with us then . . . and, we are different without him now.

Thanks, Fred

"The universe is made up of stories, not atoms."
~ Muriel Rukeyser ~

[4] https://youtu.be/e1aj6nbHaao

THE OTHER IMPORTANT INFLUENCE for me during the Modesto period, and later, was Frank Battisti. Again, the reader can find numerous books from Frank's pen, or books about his efforts and achievements. The story of his tenure at Ithaca High School is one that should be read by all serious teachers and conductors. It is a fabulous story! I probably first met Frank at one of the Midwest Clinics in Chicago, and worked with him in the CBDNA. Though the passage of all those many years has obscured many specifics and details, I still have great memories of my time with Frank. I must have met him fairly early in my career, because I have so many memories of our times in Chicago.

Figure 3: Frank Battisti

I had a practice of bringing an empty suitcase with me to Chicago. One of the great record stores of America was there ... Rose Records on Wabash Street. Frank and I spent some time there almost every year, with him telling me which was the better version of a particular Mahler symphony, or introducing me to some fabulous composer that I had not yet discovered. At Rose's, I was able to find dozens of great European recordings of wind music ... especially treasured were the recordings from the Netherlands Wind Ensemble and wind groups from Prague. One should remember that this was the period of vinyl recordings ... LPs ... and, years before Amazon. One of the great milestones in audio recording history was the release, in 1978, by Maestro Fennell and the Cleveland Symphonic Winds, of the Holst *Suites*, and a couple of other pieces, in a new "digital" format. There was a warning label on the back of the album jacket, warning listeners that damage to speakers was possible because of the acoustic properties of this new technology. Indeed, the bass drum strokes at the end of the first movement of the *E-flat Suite* rattled my speakers every time!

Close by to Rose's was Kroch and Brentano's Bookstore ... on State Street. We would go there, before or after Rose's, and Frank would introduce me to the books he thought I should read that year. I bought enough books and recordings to fill my empty suitcase ... and replenish my imagination back in Modesto, until the next year, when we would do it all over again. Frank's interests were wide ranging ... from historical events to biographies to philosophy to current events. For a while, we were both quite interested in trains and rail travel ... especially the Trans-Siberian Railway, running from Moscow to Vladivostok. We would send each other magazine or newspaper articles that we might find ... telling of someone's personal journey on that railway, or perhaps advertising for a particular trip. I remember that we both read, and discussed through letters, Paul Theroux's *The Great Railway Bazaar*. What a story that was!

As a teacher and musician, Frank was *sine qua non*. Many of the fundamental tenets of my teaching and approach to music making came from discussions and interactions with Frank. On one occasion, in a large gathering of conductors, the subject of commissioning and premiere performances came up. I remember quite distinctly a remark from Frank on that occasion, paraphrasing: "I'm tired of hearing the first performance of a composition. I'd like to hear the eighteenth performance of the piece. If it's good enough to hear the first time, it ought to be good enough to hear the eighteenth time. And, if it's not good enough to hear eighteen times, we probably don't need to hear it the first time." That thought stayed with me throughout my career . . . the goal was *good* music, not merely *new* music.

I remember watching and listening to Frank rehearse Stravinsky's *Octet for wind instruments* (1923) during a session at the 25th Anniversary of the Eastman Wind Ensemble in 1977. His understanding and realization of that score was the finest I have ever heard. His handling of the many rhythmic transitions in the piece was remarkable . . . seamless from one part to the next. That moment has stayed with me, also.

In working with conductors, Frank was always about the music . . . not gestures or gimmicks. We were able to have him at Northern Iowa for one of the Conducting Seminars we hosted for high school conductors in the state. We hosted several such events in the 80s, but were never able to build sufficient interest to allow for sustained offerings. For Frank's visit, despite abundant advertising, we were not able to gather a large number of participants. A few days before the event was scheduled, I phoned Frank and told him, with apologies, that only a few people would be attending. Frank's response was typical for him . . . "I always want to be involved in events that draw small numbers of people. Something important may be happening." Of course, it was a great success. Frank's focus was on helping the conductors to better understand the music in front of them, not merely in making better physical gestures. There were a few who attended who spoke of Frank's impact on them for many years afterward.

My friendship with Frank has been one of my most treasured. His influence on the profession is considerable. Frank gave birth to the National Wind Ensemble Conference; the first at the New England

"The universe is a single life comprising one substance and one soul."
~ Marcus Aurelius ~

Conservatory in 1970. With eight annual conferences at different universities around the country (the last in 1977), this was a major influence in the history of American bands and wind groups. It was a unique concept . . . no organizational structure, no officers, no committees, no fees . . . just a gathering of interested composers, conductors, publishers, and musicians looking to better understand the mysterious Art of Music. He also was instrumental, along with Timothy Reynish in England, and a few others, in the founding of the World Association of Symphonic Bands and Ensembles (WASBE) in 1981 in Manchester, England. The fundamental ideas and motivations of the National Wind Ensemble Conference are to be found in WASBE . . . only now on an international scale. Anyone who knows Frank, or anyone who has attended one of his workshops, will have a memorable story about him. And, I'll bet that every one of them will tell of how Frank had an impact on their life. Certainly, he was a major influence on my life and career. I will always be grateful for his presence in my life.

"A man needs a little madness . . . or else he never dares cut the rope and be free."
~ Nikos Kazantzakis ~

AS THINGS PROGRESSED in Modesto, and the world began to change ever so slightly, we tried new and creative ways of presenting concerts. We tried "Midnight Rug Concerts" in the Little Theatre on campus. The audience was invited to come at midnight . . . after dinner and other events . . . bring a rug to sit on, as well as wine and cheese, or desserts of some sort. The group, an octet, sat in a circle, with me in the middle . . . the audience sitting around the group . . . and performed music of the late 18th century *Harmoniemusik* repertoire. It was quite successful. In my last couple of years there, we also tried doing concerts earlier than the traditional 8:00 PM time. We advertised one hour concerts . . . no intermission . . . starting at 7:01 PM, and ending at 7:59 PM. "Come hear a concert . . . *then* go for dinner!" Those, also, were quite successful. In the summers, we often did concerts in one of several churches in the city, all with excellent acoustics . . . of chamber music, octets and the like. There was one occasion, during the regular academic year, when we were invited to perform at the local Mormon church . . . it was a Sunday afternoon performance. Just before the performance began, one of the church officers came to me and explained that the day was a "special" one in the Mormon calendar, and that the congregation would not be applauding that day. It was promised that they would enjoy the performance immensely, and would be grateful for our visit . . . but, no applause. It was a bit disconcerting to end a piece with a forceful ending, and hear only the silence which followed. But, as I would turn to acknowledge the audience each time, I could see huge smiles on the faces of all the people, letting us know that they were receiving our message . . . and, loving it!

In 1978, California voted into law its famous Proposition 13, a bill intended to lower (by 57%) the property taxes of homeowners. As a result of this seemingly well intentioned measure, local and state revenues plummeted. The vote was scheduled for June 6 of that year. The College immediately had a decrease of some 5,000 students, and released all of its adjunct faculty for the coming fall semester. High schools across the state dropped their art and music programs, and many gave up their athletic programs. Of course, many of these athletic programs quickly came back, as parents resolved to pay an extra fee for such programs. Years later, there were also many music programs that returned. But, the tide had turned. No longer was education "free" in California. It was then that tuition began to be instituted at the two-year colleges, and tuition was raised at the four-year institutions. For me, it seemed the right time to leave.

IN THE FALL OF 1979, I began my doctoral studies in music education at the University of Illinois in Urbana-Champaign. At that time, there were almost no doctoral conducting programs in the country . . . the idea of a "performance based" doctorate being quite a controversial idea at that time. I chose Illinois because it had the best music education doctoral program in the country. It was a superb experience, and a wonderful education. I was able to work with a brilliant faculty, and a remarkable group of doctoral students. In the first year, I was assigned to teach the beginning undergraduate courses in conducting. Later, I got to work with and conduct the Illini Symphony, an orchestra for students in all majors.

And, I spent a year as Associate Editor for the *Bulletin*, a quarterly publication of the Council for Research in Music Education.

In my second year, I was also able to study with Maestro Mircea Cristescu, Conductor of the George Enescu Philharmonic in Bucharest. The Maestro was a Visiting Professor at the University for the 1980–81 academic year. We met weekly, usually in extended sessions, which often included dinner and lengthy discussions about music. He used the same score study method which had been taught to me by Maestro Whitwell, who had been so instructed during his time at the Academy of Music in Vienna. The sessions with Maestro Cristescu helped to deepen my understanding of this study system, which allows for greater understanding of the music at hand. My year with the Maestro is remembered with great affection, and deep appreciation for his guidance.

At the end of my second year of study at Illinois, all course work was completed and I was working on my dissertation. I had interviewed for several positions that spring, but did not get an offer. Traditional assistantship awards at that time were for two years, with little chance of renewal. I interviewed for the last open position as a university wind conductor around the beginning of August ... time was running out. It was now only a few days before the beginning of classes for the fall, and I had no options. I had determined to move back to California, live with my mother, write my dissertation, and work as a drummer.

Once again, I felt at the lowest point of my life.

I stopped by the band building to say goodbye to Dr. Begian, and thank him for his encouragement and support. When I told him of my plans, he said something like, "Stay here in the office, I'll be back soon." I waited for about an hour, I suppose. When he returned, he had wrangled from the Dean a full assistantship for me ... recruiting for the School of Music, and working for the band department. When I asked what I would do for the bands, he said, "We'll figure that out." It was an incredibly fine gesture from him, a moment which changed the course of my life.

Figure 4: Harry Begian

One of my assignments that year was to organize the holdings of Albert Austin Harding, the famed Director of Bands from 1907 until 1948. The Harding Band Building was dedicated in March of 1957, and Mr. Harding died in December of that year. His office was closed, and remained unexamined until 1981. Indeed, I found a pair of white gloves on his desk when I first entered to begin my work. I catalogued and organized his many transcriptions of orchestral works which he made for the Illinois Bands. There was also a separate file made for the Chicago Symphony programs which he attended and made notes in the margins, noting his plans for a transcription. I was able to organize and create separate files for the vast correspondence which Mr. Harding had maintained with other luminaries in the band world of his time. There were letters from Percy Aldridge Grainger, John Philip Sousa, Karl King, William Revelli (Michigan), Clarence Sawhill (UCLA), Glenn Cliffe Bainum (Wisconsin), Keith Wilson (Yale), and many others. There was also a small personal library of compositions that were apparently given to Mr. Harding as gifts. It is one of my great memories that I was allowed this responsibility for organizing Mr. Harding's office.

Dr. Begian's intervention was the second time in my life that some-one had stepped in, at the precisely right moment, to keep my life headed in the direction it needed to go. The first was the mix of people and events associated with being offered the position at Modesto Junior College. There are some who would say that these are mere coincidences. For me, these were moments of destiny. Without Dr. Begian's support, I would have had almost no other options at that moment. And, with the choice I did have ... my career as a conductor might well have ended; certainly drastically altered. Though I did not spend more time with him after that year, Harry Begian remained an important figure in my life. He was an exceptional conductor and musician, and brought great passion to performances. I admired and respected him immensely. He gave me many opportunities that year that were not normally offered to doctoral candidates. Dr. Begian died in 2010, after more than fifty years as a nationally and internationally recognized band conductor and music educator.

I still miss him very much.

In each of my three years at Illinois, I was invited to interview for conducting positions at several prestigious universities. But, for one reason or another, none seemed a good "fit" for my abilities and motivations. In the spring of 1982, I was fortunate to have interviews for positions at Wake Forest University in North Carolina; Western Illinois University in Macomb, and the University of Northern Iowa. I accepted the offer from Northern Iowa . . . again, a turning point and a crossroads. From my perspective now, thirty-five years later, it was perhaps the best decision I ever made.

"I don't believe people are looking for the meaning of life as much as they are looking for the experience of being alive."
~ Joseph Campbell ~

Exposition

Beginnings at Northern Iowa

I BEGAN MY TENURE at the University of Northern Iowa (UNI) as Assistant Professor of Music, and Conductor of the Wind Ensemble, in the fall semester of 1982. My predecessor was Dr. Karl Holvik, who was a member of the faculty from 1947 until 1984. In that first year, my only assignment was to conduct the Wind Ensemble, as all other courses related to my position were still taught by Dr. Holvik. For medical reasons, he had stopped conducting the Wind Ensemble, but still held a full-time position on the faculty.

So, I had lots of time on my hands, and used that time to visit as many high schools in the state as I could. It was my intention to gather impressions of the university, and the School of Music, from high school music teachers—especially graduates of UNI. From my work in recruiting at Illinois, I had learned the importance of a carefully crafted plan for attracting good students to the university. I asked questions about our recruiting efforts ... what was working; what didn't, and their impressions of how we might form closer relationships. These visits, which I continued for several years, helped form the basis for the numerous changes we would make over the years.

"Life can only be understood backwards ... but, it must be lived forwards.
~ Søren Kierkegaard ~

The first concert with the Wind Ensemble was given on Friday 22 October 1982, at 8:00 PM in the Auditorium of Russell Hall. I wanted the repertoire for that concert to indicate a "new beginning"; to signal what I intended for the future. The program offered music from composers not normally associated with the band world—Beethoven and Wagner; there was a piece which existed at that time only in manuscript—Holst; a work for only thirteen players—Strauss, and a newer work with improvisatory passages—Paulson.

Ludwig van Beethoven	*Military March* (1816)	
Richard Wagner	*Trauermusik* (1844)	
Gustav Holst	*Moorside Suite* (1928)	
Richard Strauss	*Serenade*, op. 7 (1882)	
John Paulson	*Epinicion* (1975)	
Clifton Williams	*Symphonic Suite* (1957)	

Table 1: UNI Wind Ensemble concert repertoire, 22 October 1982

Except for the Wagner and Williams pieces, that repertoire had never been performed on our campus. The second concert that Fall was on Wednesday, 8 December ... again, as was standard at that time, at 8:00 PM in Russell Auditorium.

Tiburtio Massaino	*Canzon Trigesimaquinta* (1608)
Bastiano Chilese	*Canzon Trigesimaquarta* (1608)
Michael Praetorius	*Dance Suite from the Terpsichore* (1612)
Alec Wilder	*Walking Home in Spring* (1942)
Alec Wilder	*A Debutante's Diary* (1939)
Serge Prokofiev	*March*, op. 99 (1943)
Francis McBeth	*Kaddish* (1976)
Bozo Vojnovich	*Triptychon* (1968)

Table 2: UNI Wind Ensemble concert repertoire, 8 December 1982

And, again, with the exception of the McBeth and Prokofiev works, all were first time performances.

It was always my intention to change the name of the group to "Wind Symphony." There was no opportunity to make this change until I was actually on campus ... I felt I had to make the change quickly, while I was still in the "honeymoon" stage. After discussions with the Director of the School of Music, and several senior members of the faculty, we changed the name, effective in the Spring semester of 1983. My earlier experience in higher education, and participation in national and regional conferences of professional organizations, had given me time to consider the consequences of the name one assigns to a performing ensemble.

So, the Northern Iowa Wind Symphony gave its first performance with the new name in February of 1983, on the occasion of what was then known as the Tallcorn Band Festival. This was the first use of the term, "Wind Symphony," in the Midwest. Among other colleges and universities in the state, and the ones surrounding, the preferred names for the premier wind group of that period were Symphony Band, Symphonic Band, Wind Ensemble, Symphonic Wind Ensemble, and Concert Band. Among the faculty in the School of Music, most had little to say about the change . . . some saying something like, "I'll just call it a wind band." I don't remember much comment from the high school conductors in the state. But, a few years later, one or two high schools in the Cedar Rapids area re-named their top ensemble "Wind Symphony." Then, a couple in Des Moines. Then, one of the universities. Soon, the name was no longer uncommon.

"There are years that ask questions . . . and years that answer."
~ Zora Neale Hurston ~

After the first couple of years, the faculty were asked to provide a syllabus for each class that they taught. And, for ensembles, we were asked to provide a "mission statement," to better explain our purpose. Our mission statement, which appeared in each semester's syllabus was as follows:

Mission Statement . . .

The Wind Symphony is part of the Division of Ensembles and Conducting in the University of Northern Iowa School of Music, and has as its primary mission the preparation of instrumental-ists and conductors for professional careers in performance and education. It is our goal to provide a program that will develop well-rounded musicians who are prepared to face the challenges of an ever-changing musical world. Additionally, we are directed toward maintaining a leadership role locally, nationally, and internationally.

We wish to provide University students, staff, faculty, and the community with an avenue to continue their involvement in the performing arts. We offer opportunities for those who do not have career plans in music to develop the aesthetic self in addition to the academic self.

The Northern Iowa Wind Symphony returned to its former name, UNI Wind Ensemble, following my retirement in May of 2017.

Ensemble Personnel, Rehearsal and Performance Scheduling

PRIOR TO MY ARRIVAL, the process of student auditions for ensembles had been "ensemble specific." That is, an audition notice for each ensemble ... Wind Ensemble, Symphonic Band, and Orchestra ... was posted somewhere in the building at the beginning of each semester, and students were free to choose the ensemble(s) for which they wished to audition. These auditions were scheduled during the rehearsal times for each ensemble. So, actual rehearsals didn't start until the second week of classes. In the fall semesters of those early years, only the Wind Symphony and Orchestra were offered; with the Symphonic Band performing only in spring semesters. After several years, we started offering a "Concert Band" in the fall semesters ... for non majors; majors not assigned to the Wind Symphony or Orchestra, but who had completed their marching band requirements; and for majors who wanted experience on a secondary instrument. Around 2004, due to growth in the band program and the School of Music, we scheduled the Symphonic Band for both fall and spring semesters. And, a little after that, we also scheduled the Concert Band in the spring ... primarily as a lab ensemble for graduate conducting students. That gave us two wind groups in the fall, and three in the spring. This meant that we were able to expand our opportunities for students to perform with a "concert ensemble"—both music majors and non-majors.

With the arrival of Dr. Rebecca Burkhardt, as Director of Orchestral Activities in the fall of 1988, and with the consent of William Shepherd, Director of the Marching Band and Symphonic Band in this period, we changed our individual audition practices to a single audition process, whereby all students were auditioned in the weekend prior to the beginning of classes. So, we heard all the trumpets during one block of time, all flutes at another, etc. We felt that it was important to hear all of the players of a particular instrument in one block of time, so that we might better compare and contrast the players' abilities. Initially, we scheduled ten-minute audition slots, but as time passed and student numbers increased, we shortened those times to seven minutes. And, at first, students could choose the ensemble in which they wished to perform, assuming they met the performance standards of that particular ensemble. Again, with the passage of time, we realized that some, if not many, students were missing important musical experiences in choosing to be part of the same ensemble each semester. So, after a few years, we changed the policy so that students were assigned to ensembles based on the audition results. The audition form was changed to indicate in which ensembles, and which semesters, each student had performed. Our goal was to make sure that every wind and percussion student had both a band experience, and an orchestral experience during their tenure in the School of Music. Because of individual student ability and progress with their performing skills, it was not always possible to realize our goal. But, we came pretty close.

I should also mention that the Jazz Bands held separate auditions during the first week of classes. So, there was a delay in knowing to which ensembles students were assigned. Students were required to perform in one ensemble each semester until the required number of credits for their degree was attained. Depending on their abilities and desires, students also had the option of performing in two ensembles each semester. Again, after a few years of this glitch in the process, we decided to schedule auditions for the Jazz Bands at the same time as the other ensemble auditions . . . the three days prior to the beginning of classes in the fall. So, trumpets, trombones, and saxophones were scheduled in such a way that they would audition for the concert ensembles at a specifically assigned time, and then go to the jazz auditions a half hour or so earlier or later . . . again, at a specified time. This change made the whole process much easier. It meant that all auditions were completed in the same time period, and ensemble rehearsals could begin on the first day of classes each semester.

"People who lean on logic and philosophy and rational exposition end by starving the best part of their minds."
~ William Butler Yeats ~

WITH REGARD TO NUMBER of players assigned to the Wind Symphony, there were several factors involved in that decision. Certainly, we wanted to make sure that all the ensembles could function and perform appropriate repertoire. So, we needed players in all sections for all ensembles. The number of students in a particular studio was a factor. Ideally, we needed at least nine bassoon players to fill the needs of three ensembles ... Wind Symphony, Orchestra, and Symphonic Band. That was not always possible. In some years, for different reasons, there were low numbers on a particular instrument. The following year, those numbers might rebound, but we might have fewer of another instrument. We finally learned to "share" players who might only be needed for a particular work on a single program. For instance, when the Wind Symphony, normally having five or six percussionists, needed eight players for a particular piece, we could have those extra players only come for those rehearsals for which they were needed. Those "extra" players were indicated on the "Ensemble Assignments" notice posted after auditions each semester.

Flute	5 (2,2, piccolo)
Oboe/English Horn	3 (1,1, English horn)
Bassoon	3 (1,1, contrabassoon)
Clarinet	10-11 (3,3,3, E-flat, bass clarinet)
Saxophone	4 (2 alto [soprano], tenor, baritone)
Horn	5 (2,1,1,1)
Trumpet	6 (2,2,2 or some combination of cornets and trumpets)
Trombone	4 (2,1,1)
Euphonium	2
Tuba	2-3
Percussion	5-6
Harp	
Piano	
Contrabass	

Table 3: Ideal instrumentation for the UNI Wind Symphony

Of course, in many years, it was not possible to have three oboists ... or five horns ... or one or more of the auxiliary instruments (harp, piano, contrabass). In the early years, we had only six to eight clarinets. In the last few years, because of the large number of fine saxophonists, we assigned five players to the group. There was one year when there were only three trombonists in the school. Somehow, we were able to share those three players among the Wind Symphony, Orchestra, and Jazz Band One. That was a difficult year! But, mostly, the numbers indicated above remained fairly consistent over the thirty-five years of the Wind Symphony's existence.

ANOTHER PRACTICE which was instituted upon my arrival was the policy of "player rotation." This meant that, within the limitations and abilities of individual players . . . all players would be assigned to first, second, and third parts for each concert. So, that meant that every clarinet player could expect to play the first part on at least one piece for each concert. As we were an educational institution, I felt that all students should have a varied performing experience. I believed it in their best interests that they have experiences with the more challenging first parts . . . *and*, learn how to play as part of a team on a lower part. Initially, this idea was not fully possible . . . there were just some players who did not have the ability to play first parts. But, over the years, things got better and better. By the start of the new millennium or so, the practice worked for every section. I must admit that there was some resistance to this policy among the students in the first two or three years. There were a few who had "always played first," and looked on this new practice as insulting. And, those players who had usually played lower parts experienced some anxiety when assigned to a higher part. But, we got better each year. After a few years, most students could not imagine another way of doing things. This practice of rotating players among parts was eventually adopted by both the Symphony Orchestra and Symphonic Band.

"One day's exposure to mountains is better than cartloads of books."
~John Muir ~

I also wanted each player to have experience on every instrument in their family. Again, as our primary mission was that of preparing and educating students for careers in the music profession, I believed that a varied experience with similar instruments to be helpful in their growth and maturity. Of course, it took a few years for this practice to take full effect. Saxophonists could expect to play all the instruments for each concert ... alto, tenor, baritone, and occasionally soprano. Clarinet players were assigned E-flat and bass, sometimes contra, parts. After a while, I realized that clarinet and saxophone players need some time to change instruments between pieces, and that they often had to bring several instruments to rehearsals and performances. So, after discussions with the players and their teachers, we revised the practice so that players were assigned instruments only for each concert or half of a concert, rather than for each piece. So, a clarinetist might be assigned to play bass clarinet on the first half, and E-flat on the second half. A saxophonist might play alto on the first half, and baritone in the second part. This practice seemed to work well for everyone.

Trumpet players played both trumpet and cornet, and occasionally a specialty instrument like piccolo trumpet or flugelhorn. All flute players played piccolo on at least one piece in each concert. As with player rotation, this was not a popular idea with students in the early years. There was some fear attached to playing a different instrument, even though the embouchure and fingerings were almost the same. Of course, achieving a characteristic sound on each instrument offered a different challenge. It was here that I appreciated the support and assistance of our studio faculty in helping the students to broaden their abilities and possibilities. And, as with player rotation, after some years of this practice, students came to value the opportunity to expand their abilities and experiences, and could not imagine another way.

WHEN WE FIRST STARTED in the fall semester, 1982, rehearsals for the Wind Symphony were scheduled on Mondays from 4:00 PM until 5:50 PM, and Wednesdays from 6:00 PM until 7:50 PM. The Orchestra rehearsed at the same times, but reversed days. At that time, the legal drinking age in Iowa was eighteen, and the Student Center on campus served beer. So, by the time of our rehearsals, especially Wednesdays, many students had already started "happy hour." This, of course, made rehearsals difficult. There was also some illegal drug use among students, though not wide spread. The previous practice had been that students started to arrive at the appointed hour; the rehearsal actually starting about fifteen minutes after the hour. After the first week of this, I announced that rehearsals would begin promptly on the hour. Further, those not in their assigned seat and ready to play at the appointed time would be considered late, and this would affect their semester grade. I also began to lock the doors to the rehearsal hall at the appointed hour, causing students to not be allowed in after rehearsals started. This, of course, caused anger and frustration among the students. This new wrinkle in proceedings, along with the other changes indicated above, gave cause for some students in the group to circulate a petition, calling for my dismissal. Luckily, the Director of the School of Music believed that I was on pretty firm ground. But, it was not a time without frustration and adversity.

I gave my attention and support mostly to freshmen and graduate students … believing that they were the future of the ensemble, as they had no experience with previous practice. Their support, along with the quality of the music we were rehearsing and performing, helped to turn things around. It would be several years before the group really started to "gel," and we began to find our sense of community. But, by the second semester of that first year, I knew that we were on the right track.

With all the changes in the practices and policies of the ensemble, rehearsals were further complicated by the fact that they were scheduled so late in the day. Students were simply too tired to give their full attention to rehearsals. And, other events … recitals and concerts … started immediately after rehearsals; at 6:00 PM and 8:00 PM. After a few years, much discussion, and some teeth gnashing among the faculty, we were able to successfully create a new class schedule that allowed for ensemble rehearsals as follows:

Time	Monday	Tuesday	Wednesday	Thursday
1:00–2:50	WS	Jazz Bands	WS	Jazz Bands
3:10–5:00	Orch	Sym Band	Orch	Sym Band

Table 4: UNI rehearsal schedule

This made almost everything much easier. Again, though the previous schedule had existed for many, many years, I'm sure that present day students ... and faculty ... would have difficulty in imagining another way.

WE ESTABLISHED A PATTERN of public performances that remained fairly consistent throughout the years. The Scholarship Benefit Concert was the first event of the academic year, and was scheduled for the last weekend in September. When I first arrived, this event was scheduled for the spring semester, but was soon changed to the fall. It was a special event, obviously intended to raise much needed scholarship funds, and included performances to represent all areas of the School of Music. This generally meant that the Wind Symphony was on the program, often with a student or faculty soloist; the Symphony Orchestra; Jazz Band One; one or more of the choral ensembles, and faculty artists.

We tried to schedule the first performance for the Wind Symphony alone on the first Friday of October. Initially, only the Wind Symphony performed, but later we started to share the program with the Symphonic Band. I always wanted to schedule concerts for Friday evenings, to make it a little easier for parents, alumni, and other interested patrons, to make the drive to Cedar Falls. That generally worked well when all performances were in the Auditorium of Russell Hall (the music building). But, when the new Performing Arts Center (PAC) opened in 2000, it became more difficult to schedule Friday performances. This was, of course, due to having to share the Great Hall with performances offered by the PAC management, and other civic groups.

The second concert was usually scheduled in the week prior to Thanksgiving break. As most all of the large ensembles were trying to get their performances scheduled around the same time, that often made it difficult to schedule a Friday performance. As much as possible, I tried to avoid performances during the week as those inevitably drew a smaller audience ... and I didn't like the idea of having students putting their heart and soul into the performance, and then having to return to their dorm room and prepare for classes the next day . . . or another performance.

In the spring, the band festival was always scheduled for the second full weekend of February[5] and the Wind Symphony always performed on the Friday night of that event. I always considered this an important performance as the audience included forty or fifty high school band directors, and around two hundred of the best young musicians in the state. This was an important part of our recruiting efforts.

[5] For more on the Band Festival see pages 75–79.

For several years, we scheduled another concert in the week prior to Spring Break in mid-March. This was especially helpful in those years in which we took a European concert tour. It made things easier when we could perform the tour program at home, before performing for the audiences in Hungary and Italy. But, it became more and more difficult to schedule around that time, so we dropped that. The final concert was always scheduled in April. Again, April was a popular month for performances, and it was quite difficult to schedule a concert among all the other ensembles needing to find a date. Indeed, our final performance in 2017 was initially scheduled for Friday 21 April at Urbandale High School, as there was no date available in the Great Hall. Later, it was made possible for us to do a second performance of the program in the Great Hall on the following Monday.

So, in summary, we generally did five or six performances each year . . . usually five to six weeks apart. There were also four or five performances each year by the Chamber Wind Players, a small ensemble to be discussed in the next section. In the first few years, there were also concert tours around the state during spring break.[6]

[6] See the chapter, Concert Tours.

Repertoire

I CONSIDER THE SELECTION OF REPERTOIRE to be at the very
heart of the ensemble experience ... indeed, repertoire is the only
reason to have an ensemble. One's choices for repertoire are a reflection of the conductor's values and attitudes regarding the nature
and intention of music; the essence and purpose of education, and
the role of the ensemble in the larger profession. In an educational
institution (secondary school or university), the music that the
conductor selects for study and performance becomes, *de facto*, the
curriculum for those students. I believe that one should seek music
of the highest aesthetic value possible; music that has the capacity
to stir one's emotions, and produce catharsis ... a cleansing of the
soul ... in both the performer and the listener. We should choose
the best music possible for our students, within their present abilities and level of maturity. Eugene Corporon once observed that ...
with regard to repertoire ... "every act of acceptance is also an act
of rejection." That is, in choosing any composition ... or group of
compositions ... for performance, the conductor is also rejecting all
other compositions available. For this ensemble; for these students;
for this occasion ... that conductor is proclaiming, in effect, the
selected pieces to be the finest available. Some may wish to argue
with this assertion. But, the essence is correct—choosing repertoire
is serious business.

I believe strongly in the idea of a "core repertoire," a body of works
that represent the history of the wind medium, which extends
back to the Renaissance and beyond. This repertoire should include

*"If I can get out of the way, if I can be pure enough,
if I can be selfless enough, and if I can be generous
and loving and caring enough to abandon what
I have and my own preconceived, silly notions
of what I think I am ... and become truly who
in fact I am, which is really just another child of
God ... then the music can really use me. And,
therein lies my fulfillment. That's when the music
starts to happen.*
~John McLaughlin ~

representative works from the best composers of each period ...
Renaissance, Baroque, Classic, Nineteenth Century Romantic, and
Twentieth Century (early, middle, late) ... those which exemplify
the finest characteristics of a particular period. And, the music
should, primarily, be originally composed for ensembles of wind
instruments. Indeed, music from the Renaissance through the late
seventeenth century was a fertile period for ensembles of wind instruments. From this period, we have the great sonatas and canzoni
from Gabrieli and his contemporaries. Tielman Susato left us his
dance music collection for ensembles of wind instruments. At the
close of the Renaissance, and beginning of the Baroque, we have the
extraordinary collection of dance music from Michael Praetorius ...
the *Terpsichore*. It was only after the great improvements in string
instruments at the beginning of the seventeenth century that string
ensembles begin to rise to primacy.

Throughout my tenure at Northern Iowa, I endeavored to make
sure that every student who went through our program ... over a
four-year period ... would study and perform works by outstanding
composers, representing every musical period in which music for
ensembles of wind instruments was composed. Within the limits
of time and resources, students should be given the opportunity
to study and perform the best music from each musical period.
For example, every brass student should have performed music
of Gabrieli ... or other representative composers ... during their
undergraduate tenure. Clarinets, oboes, bassoons, and horns
should know, and perform, the wind music of Mozart, and/or
one of the other very fine composers of that period who wrote for
Harmoniemusik. We should include the wind music of Berlioz,
Wagner, Dvořák, and Strauss from the nineteenth century. All
students should have the opportunity to study and perform the
music from Gustav Holst and the English School as part of their
education. They should know the music of Percy Aldridge Grainger.
They should have performed works from Karel Husa and Paul
Hindemith ... and, works from David Maslanka, Ron Nelson, and
David Gillingham. Simply put, there are masterpieces from every
musical epoch that students should study and perform during their
time in our care. They study Mozart in history classes, and they

analyze Mozart in theory classes ... they should perform Mozart
in our ensembles. And, by that, I mean the music which Mozart
composed originally for wind instruments ... not a transcription
for modern band of an opera overture. Obviously, there is not
original music from all historical periods for each instrument.
Saxophones were perhaps the last instrument to be added to the
modern wind orchestra, coming to us in the mid-nineteenth
century. So, Mozart would not be appropriate for them. But, French
wind music from the second half of the nineteenth century might
be excellent.

In the early years, there was not much chamber music performed
in the School of Music. There was the Tuba/Euphonium ensemble,
the Percussion Ensembles, the Flute Choir, and Horn Choir ... but
these were ensembles with discrete instrumentation; there was no
ensemble performing chamber music with a diverse instrumentation. So, in the beginning, I programmed music for the Wind
Symphony concerts which I believed important for our students'
education ... regardless of the number of players needed. Thus,
the reader will notice Richard Strauss' *Serenade* op. 7, and chamber
works from Alec Wilder on the first two concerts in 1982. But, as
we moved forward, I came to realize that in programming chamber works with the Wind Symphony, I was leaving out too many
students who needed valuable rehearsal and performing experience. For example, the Strauss *Serenade* uses only 2 flutes, 2 oboes, 2
bassoons, 2 clarinets, 4 horns, and a contrabass. So, around 1985, I
formed a separate ensemble which was named the Chamber Wind
Players. That group met on Fridays for two hours. The goal was
to perform music for large chamber ensembles ... octet, nonet,
double quintet, brass group, etc ... that required a conductor. The
group normally performed two concerts each semester, though
we sometimes shared a concert with another chamber group ...
strings, tuba group, flute choir, etc. The repertoire was primarily music composed in the eighteenth and nineteenth centuries,
though there were also pieces from the Renaissance, Baroque, and
twentieth centuries.

We discontinued this ensemble around 2012, when there was not
a sufficient number of players on certain instruments to schedule
the ensemble ... without overburdening those players and their
commitments to other ensembles. And, as new teachers joined
the faculty, there were more people who believed strongly in the
need for chamber music as part of each student's education. The
Trombone Choir and Clarinet Choir were formed, as well as saxophone ensembles (quartets, quintets). And, faculty put together
ensembles, with themselves and one of their better students, in performances of works such as Mozart's *Gran Partita*, K. 361/370a, and
Dvořák's *Serenade* op. 44. Two or three rehearsals were scheduled,
and then a performance. No need for a special weekly rehearsal
time, throughout the semester. Still, something special ... and
important to the education of our students ... was lost with the
elimination of the Chamber Wind Players.

I also believed it important that students perform newly composed
works, especially pieces composed by the more substantial of contemporary composers. I do not subscribe to the idea of performing
a work solely on the basis that it is newly composed. I always asked
myself, "Would I want to perform this piece again in a few years?" If
my answer was no, I probably didn't perform it at all. Remembering
the lesson learned from Maestro Battisti ... it wasn't so much that
I sought to find *new* music, as much as I was determined to find
good music. For concert programs, I tried to find a healthy balance
between pieces from the "core repertoire," and newly composed
pieces.

And, I believed it important that we perform music by composers
from other countries. Thus, I took it upon myself to learn as much
as possible about fine composers from other countries who composed for the wind orchestra. This involved two sabbaticals (called
"professional development leaves" at UNI) ... in 1991, and again
in 2001 ... and my Fulbright experience in Hungary during the
2004–2005 academic year. I also became involved with international organizations such as the World Association for Symphonic
Bands and Ensembles (WASBE), and the Internationale Gesellschaft
zur Erforschung und Förderung der Blasmusik (IGEB). Attending

conferences for such organizations gave me excellent opportunities to hear wind music from other countries, meet composers and conductors, and establish relationships with them. Especially in the early years ... before the internet and cyberspace ... these events were crucial in discovering what might be available in other parts of the planet. From 1991 until 2017, I traveled internationally almost every year, sometimes two or three visits per year. From these visits, I was able to know ... and, perform ... excellent works from composers in Hungary, the Czech Republic, Italy, Spain, England, Germany, the Netherlands, Israel, Belgium, Latvia, Estonia, Japan, and a few others.

"I watched the trees gradually withdraw, waving their despairing arms, seeming to say to me, 'What you fail to learn from us today, you will never know. If you allow us to drop back into the hollow of this road from which we sought to raise ourselves up to you, a whole part of yourself which we were bringing to you will fall forever into the abyss.'"

~ Marcel Proust ~

Over the years, we developed three categories of repertoire:

1. Performance Repertoire
    ... music designated for performance in the season. With four to six pieces for each concert, we could usually perform twenty-five to thirty pieces each season. And, with the Chamber Wind Players being offered for more than twenty-five years, there was another twenty-five to thirty pieces each year.

2. Rehearsal Repertoire
    ... pieces that were rehearsed on a somewhat regular basis, but not performed. These were simpler pieces, grade II or III, and chosen for their expressive qualities. These are at the beginning of rehearsals, and allowed us to begin to "feel" the ensemble, and start to listen closely ... within each section, and across the ensemble. As there were few technical demands in these pieces, we were able to reinforce our communication abilities, and begin to behave as a single entity, rather than fifty individuals.

3. Reading Repertoire
    ... works that were distributed for a read-through, and collected at the end of rehearsal. These were pieces that I felt that students needed to know about, but didn't make it in the selection process for performance. These were often marches, both American and European; pieces that graduate conducting students were learning, and pieces sent to me from composers or friends in other countries. This repertoire also included composers such as

Clare Grundman, Francis McBeth, Clifton Williams, and other
fine composers from that period.

This concept of three differing sets of repertoire allowed us to have
experience ... some greater, some lesser ... with fifty to sixty
pieces of music each year. Of course, this took about twenty-five
years to develop. Certainly, this practice would not have been
possible in the early years. But, over time, as we started to attract
better prepared students, and traditions of performance excellence
began to emerge in the ensemble, we were able to expand our
possibilities for students to learn and experience more repertoire.
To my mind, that is always a good thing!

Still, with all my efforts toward ensuring that our students received
a comprehensive and balanced education through the repertoire
we performed, there were still gaps in our offerings. We were never
able to have the requisite number of "solo" players needed for a
performance of David Maslanka's *A Child's Garden of Dreams* ... a
work which I consider to be one of the finest compositions, for any
medium, of the late twentieth century. One of the few regrets I
carry from my tenure at Northern Iowa is that we were not able
to perform this magnificent composition. For the same reason,
we were never able to mount a performance of Michael Colgrass'
Winds of Nagual, another masterpiece. There was no performance
of Stravinsky's *Octet* or the *Symphonies of Wind Instruments.* We were
not able to perform Mr. Husa's *Concerto for Wind Orchestra.* There
were several other pieces of substantial aesthetic value, from world-
class composers, that we simply were not able to perform, due to
the lack of sufficient players with the technical skills needed for
meaningful performances.

While there were several major works that we were not able to
perform ... for one reason or another ... we *did* give our energies to
many of the lesser known works of Grainger and Holst, along with
a few others. And, in developing my relationships with composers
in Hungary, Germany, Italy, Israel, and other countries, we were
able to perform some extraordinary music not well known by many
American conductors.

CENTRAL TO OUR HISTORY was the great Australian composer, Percy Aldridge Grainger (1882–1961). He had an enormous influence on the music world ... composing for most every medium. I consider Percy to be one of the very finest composers who wrote extensively for the wind medium ... in many ways, far superior to the other band composers of his time. In our history, there were fifty-six performances of twenty different compositions from Grainger's pen ... *Colonial Song, The Gumsuckers, Children's March*, and *Molly on the Shore* being the most favored. Except for my sabbatical and Fulbright years, we performed at least one work of Percy's almost every year. Because many of Grainger's works are shorter one-movement pieces ... often from folk material ... I usually put two or three together to make a sort of "suite," making sure to have some variety in tempo, texture, and emotional tone. Only late in my tenure did I discover his *Suite on Danish Folk Songs*, published in an "elastic scoring" version by Schott/Schirmer around 1930. There are four movements: "The Power of Love," "Lord Peter's Stable Boy," "The Nightingale and the Two Sisters," and "Jutish Medley." To my mind, this is one of Grainger's most inspired works ... in many ways, more musically satisfying than *Lincolnshire Posy*. I should also mention his *Lads of Wamphray* and *Marching Song of Democracy* as among his finest works.

Figure 5: Percy Aldridge Grainger

DANIEL BUKVICH (b. 1954) is a composer who also figures prominently in the history of the Wind Symphony. I first became aware of Dan in the summer of 1989. Our tuba/euphonium professor had been a member of the summer faculty at the University of Illinois summer music camp, and had heard one of Dan's works on the final concert ... a "theatre piece" entitled *Voodoo*. From the description of the piece, it seemed like a work that would be excellent for our students. I contacted Gary Green, Conductor at the University of Miami, who had been the guest conductor at the Illinois music camp. He had many good things to say about Dan, and gave me his phone number. (Again, this was a time before computers and cell phones.) I called Dan, and we talked for quite a while. We performed *Voodoo* for the first time on 8 December 1989. That was the start of a beautiful relationship!

Figure 6: Daniel Bukvich

Dan and I stayed in touch (by phone!). He sent me several scores of other of his compositions . . . all of which I liked very much. In the next few years, we performed his *Maine Vigils; Surprise, Pattern, and Illusion,* and the *Hymn of St. Francis.* Our first Concert Tour in Hungary was scheduled for March of 1993. I called Dan, and asked if he had anything new that I might take with us for the concert program. He said no, but offered to compose a work especially for the occasion. The result was *The Dream of Abraham,* one of Dan's finest works.[7] At the request and instigation of Jeffrey Funderburk, our Professor of Tuba, Dan also composed a work for solo tuba and wind orchestra for our 1996 return to Hungary . . . *Meditations on the Writings of Vasily Kandinsky.*[8] And, for our final concert tour in Hungary in March of 2000, we took along Dan's *Unusual Behavior in Ceremonies Involving Drums.* Though not composed specifically for the Wind Symphony, we performed the revised version of the work originally commissioned by Kappa Kappa Psi National Band Fraternity.

Over the years, we performed several other of Dan's fabulous compositions . . . twenty performances of twelve different compositions. Many of our performances can be heard on his website. We were able to have Dan on our campus on two different occasions for the Northern Festival of Bands, our annual event for high school students. Dan came as guest conductor, and performed his own compositions. These were two of our most successful festivals during my thirty-five year tenure. In his last visit, in 2016, I told him about my decision to retire from the university in the spring of 2017. Dan said that he would like to compose a piece in honor of my retirement. I was thrilled! The work he gave us is entitled *Symphonic Movement.* It is a piece in which all the sections of the ensemble . . . flute, double reed, clarinet, saxophone, trumpet, horn, trombone, tuba/euphonium, and percussion . . . have solo passages. It opens with solos in flute and alto saxophone . . . memorized and occurring in different parts of the hall . . . and, in the second part, dispersing the different sections to other locations in the hall. The work ends with a massive chorale that lifts the audience right out of their seats! Extraordinary music![9] I consider Dan Bukvich to be one of the most talented composers alive today.

[7] More on the *The Dream of Abraham* in chapter, Concert Tours.

[8] More on *Meditations on the Writings of Vasily Kandinsky* in the chapter, Concert Tours.

[9] You can find our video performance of that concert on YouTube.
`https://youtu.be/8n08WDbyfVY`

Frigyes Hidas (1928–2007), one of the most famous composers
in Hungary, composed two pieces for us. *Almost B.A.C.H.* was premiered in April of 1994 . . . a gift after our concert tour in Hungary
in March of 1993. The *Concertino for Wind Orchestra* was part of the
repertoire for that tour, a work Mr. Hidas had composed in 1981.
The *Fantasy for Violoncello and Wind Orchestra* was premiered in April
1999 with Jonathan Chenoweth as soloist. This piece was the result of my request that he compose a work for solo cello and small
wind group . . . around fifteen players. As we talked about it during
dinner one evening, he wrote the principal theme on a piece of
scratch paper, and slid it across the table to me, saying, "it will be
a one-movement piece in several sections. This will be the theme."
Already, he had it composed in his mind. That scrap of paper is
saved in one of my journals from that period. The instrumentation
for the piece was to become standard for the other concerto/solo
pieces he composed later . . . for clarinet, oboe, bassoon, violin, and
the Double Concerto for oboe and bassoon soloists.

Figure 7: Frigyes Hidas

Figure 8: Frigyes Hidas, sketch of the theme
of *Fantasy for Violoncello and Wind Orchestra*

One of our most memorable performances was the American
premiere of his *Requiem* in November of 1996. This was a piece that
I had requested from him during one of the many occasions for
dinner with Mr. Hidas and László Marosi, my long-time friend,
at the Arany Szarvas (Golden Deer) restaurant beneath the castle

on the Buda side of Budapest. We always talked about music on these occasions, as I was so keen to know more of the Hungarian musical life, and to introduce more of his music to America. With the fall of communism in 1989, the compositions of Mr. Hidas (Frici Bácsi ... Uncle Freddie ... as he was known among close friends) were starting to be well known in other European countries, and a couple of pieces were known in America. During one of the many dinners we enjoyed together with László, I asked him if he would consider composing a requiem for wind orchestra, chorus, and SATB soloists. He was very quiet for a moment, and gently said, "I have been waiting twenty-five years for someone to ask me for this ... yes, I will do it." His father had been the music director at St. Stephen's Basilica, the most important church in Budapest, maybe all of Hungary. During the communist period, the religious life in Hungary had been suppressed, and Frici missed that spirit. Now, he had a reason to have it in his life again. The premiere was given in St. Stephen's in the spring of 1996, with Maestro Marosi conducting. We gave the American premiere a few months later ... it is music of great profundity. Mr. Hidas passed away in March of 2007, only a month before my mother died. The deaths of both of them took a part of me with them. But, they left a part of their souls with me. And, that has made a difference.

The Wind Symphony performed eighteen different compositions of Maestro Hidas, with the *Requiem, Pictures of South Africa, Circus Suite, Concertino for Wind Orchestra,* and *Merry Music* being among his best offerings. There are three short videos that were made after Frici died ... reflections from friends and colleagues who knew him well.[10]

[10] The links are:
https://youtu.be/TBL7TrXzJms
https://youtu.be/WrNqWyINtCM
https://youtu.be/leI61YPjMSI

THE OTHER COMPOSER FROM HUNGARY, who was important
to both me ... and the Wind Symphony ... was Kamilló Lendvay.
He was born in 1928 ... the same year as his friend and fellow
composer, Frigyes Hidas. The two of them attended the Liszt
Academy of Music, grew up together; eventually became members
of the faculty there, and emerged as perhaps the two leading
contemporary composers of late twentieth-century Hungary.

I met Mr. Lendvay in 1991, during my first visit to Hungary. Both
he and Mr. Hidas were very kind to me, and opened many doors
to the Hungarian music community. From 1991 until 2007, I made
about twenty-five visits to Hungary, including three tours with
the Wind Symphony. Kamilló and Frigyes were always part of my
visits, and helped arrange many of the concerts for the tours. We
performed several of Kamilló's pieces for wind orchestra ... the
Festspiel Overture, composed for the 1984 Uster International Music
Festival in Switzerland; the *Concertino for Piano, Winds, Percussion, and
Harp* with Robin Guy in 1996, and again with Hungarian pianist,
András Körtesi in 2008; *Three Carnival Masks*, and the American
premiere of his *Concerto for Trumpet* with Randy Grabowski in
1994 ... Kamilló was present for that occasion. His final work for
the wind medium was his *Second Suite for Wind Orchestra*. It is a five-
movement work dedicated to five of his best friends ... a "Postcard"
for László Marosi; "Almost Hidas" for Frici, (based on the pitches
b-natural, d, a, and e-flat ... H das ... "almost" Hidas); a "Polka" for
James Croft, former conductor at Florida State (and, a graduate of
UNI); the "Finale" for Felix Hauswirth, Swiss conductor and director
of the Uster Festival. The second movement was dedicated to me ...
"A Romantic Story."

I have many wonderful memories of Mr. Lendvay. Especially in
the early visits to Hungary, he was so kind to show me around
Budapest. He once took me to the small, picturesque village of
Szentendré (Saint Andrew), outside Budapest. It was there that he
introduced me to a wonderful drink known as "Aszú." The Tokaji
grape is peculiar to the northeast region of Hungary ... it was Louis
the XIV, the French "Sun King," who once proclaimed Tokaji wine
as the "King of Wines, and the Wine of Kings." After the wine is

Figure 9: Kamilló Lendvay

produced, the remains are fermented for a bit longer, and make a sort of brandy ... Aszú. Fabulous! He took me to the castle district on many occasions, and we always had great dinners together. Very often, Frici Bacsí would join us for dinner ... the two of them together was an unforgettable experience ... every time! In 1999, I took my mother to Hungary for her one and only European visit ... at Christmas time. Mr. Lendvay, and his lovely wife, Marcsi ... a former member of the State Operetta chorus ... prepared a special Christmas Day dinner for us ... it was wonderful! Kamilló prepared a special "menu" card for the occasion, though I have since lost it. But, I am sure that the meal was one of Hungarian traditional dishes, and sweet desserts. I can almost taste it now!

Kamilló died at the end of November in 2016 ... only a couple of weeks before the passing of Karel Husa. He was an eminently kind and gentle soul, and I loved him very much. In a society which now places so much importance on technology, and increasingly provides an avenue to isolation, rather than community, I believe myself quite fortunate to have had the human experiences I did; transformative experiences then which have evolved into warm and tender memories now. Both he and Frici Bácsi doted on me when I was there ... making sure that I always had a memorable occasion. Their love and care, of course, caused me to fall in love with Hungary. I will always love Hungary ... her history; her spirit, and her people. It is my second home, and today I miss her terribly. I was fortunate to have Mr. Lendvay and Frici Bácsi in my life ... I knew it then; I know it now. We were all richer from their presence, and are poorer in their absence.

"We cannot get grace from gadgets."
~ J.B. Priestley ~

KAREL HUSA was a major figure in our history. As noted earlier, I first met Mr. Husa while living and teaching in California. The occasion was in the summer of 1973, when I was, again, invited to teach at the University of Southern California summer program in the mountains of Idyllwild. Mr. Husa had been invited to come for a week; to be present for a performance of his *Apotheosis of this Earth*. Dr. Whitwell was conducting the wind ensemble during his visit. My task was to get Mr. Husa to and from rehearsals, and generally take care of logistics. Side story ... When I was first starting in the profession, I was quite taken with the music of Hector Berlioz. It turned out that Mr. Husa was also a great fan of Berlioz, having conducted his *Requiem*[11] at Cornell (I have a vinyl disc recording of that performance!). When I first collected him at the airport for the Idyllwild visit, we then had a lengthy drive in the mountains. I started to speak of Berlioz and his music, and apparently became quite animated. At one point, during a particularly tight hairpin turn, Karel exclaimed, "Ronald, the mountain!!" We made it safely! Sometime later, in a letter making plans to meet at a conference, he wrote, "I will have no trouble finding you. I will look for the only conductor who looks like Berlioz!!" I loved it! This was to be my first of many occasions with Mr. Husa ... he became one of the most important people in my life. Over the years, we visited together on many occasions at national conferences, and maintained a fairly regular correspondence. His letters were always so personal, telling me of both personal professional events in his life, but also what he was thinking and feeling about things. I could always "feel" his presence in his writing. I think I have about fifty or so letters, both typed and handwritten, from him.

In November of 1991, he was invited to our campus as part of the Meryl Norton Hearst Endowed Chair program. Mr. Husa was on campus for a week of rehearsals and performances of his music ... ending with a performance of several of his compositions for various instruments, voices, and ensembles. We had also scheduled a special performance of his *Apotheosis of this Earth* for the annual

Figure 10: Karel Husa

[11] Berlioz, *Grande Messe des morts*, op. 5 (1837)

conference of the Iowa Music Educators Association (IMEA) in
Ames, Iowa ... this scheduled at the end of his residency week with
us. Mr. Husa had prepared a special version of the piece to include
a full SATB chorus. In the original version, the players in the ensemble have speaking parts in certain places of the third movement:
"Postscript." The first two movements of this programmatic work,
"Apotheosis" and "Tragedy of Destruction," depict the violence and
horror of the destruction of our planet ... through war, pollution
of the air and water, forest fires, and other man-made disasters. In
the final movement, the players ... emulate a faltering computer
voice attempting to utter its final message: "this beautiful earth." It
is a breathtaking ending to one of the most profound works of the
latter half of the twentieth century. In the revised version, Mr. Husa
adds a full chorus as an additional color in the thick texture of the
first two movements ... primarily vocal sounds without text. In the
final movement, the chorus takes the part spoken by the players in
the original version. The Concert Chorale and UNI Singers joined
the Wind Symphony for this once-in-a-lifetime performance ...
about two hundred musicians on stage. Actually, we gave a performance in Russell Hall Auditorium on the Friday before Mr. Husa
arrived, and had prepared for a second performance, with Mr. Husa
conducting, at the IMEA Conference.

Mr. Husa and I drove to Ames on the Thursday evening before the
scheduled Friday performance. That night was one of the worst
snow storms ever, virtually paralyzing the state. The buses, to
bring the students to Ames on Friday morning, were not able to get
out of their barns. Roads were closed; everything was shut down.
Mr. Husa did a hastily scheduled lecture about his music, and the
Apotheosis in particular, for the conference audience. Later that
afternoon, with the roads cleared and temperatures rising, I drove
him to the Des Moines airport for his flight back to Ithaca, New
York.

"No snowflake ever falls in the wrong place."
~Zen Koan ~

I have often reflected on those days, and am quite pleased that our
students and faculty were able to know this remarkable human
being ... if only for a short time. But, I was saddened that we were

not able to perform his wonderful music for that audience ... their only chance, ever, to hear this version.

Still, we were able to perform the original score five other times ... the last being in November of 2016, a little less than a month before he died. It was a brilliant performance ... quite poignant for me, as I knew it would be my final occasion to conduct his music. After that concert, I wrote a letter to Mr. Husa, again telling him what he had meant to my life; how important he was to the world, and how he had influenced so many in our profession. I included many short messages and remembrances from the students, regarding their experiences with his music. I sent it only a few days before he died. It is unclear as to whether or not he ever saw our message.

I hope so.

Throughout our history, the music of Karel Husa was part of our traditions. There were eighteen performances of his music in those thirty-five years. There were five performances of the *Apotheosis* ... in 1988, 1991, 2003, 2010, and 2016. Other of his works in our repertoire include *Music for Prague, 1968; Concerto for Percussion and Wind Ensemble: Divertimento for Brass and Percussion,* and the *Smetana Fanfare.*

I consider Mr. Husa to be one of the most important composers of the late twentieth century. His works for wind instruments came at a time when we (the profession) were first beginning to assert the wind orchestra as a legitimate musical ensemble, worthy of serious consideration as a medium for aesthetic contemplation. *Music for Prague, 1968* ... his first piece for the wind orchestra ... burst forth on the musical world as a spiritual harbinger of what was to come from this humble and gentle spirit. It is believed that there have been more than ten thousand performances of the work, worldwide ... perhaps, making it the most performed composition of the twentieth century. The *Apotheosis* appeared a couple of years later, followed by concertos for saxophone, trumpet, percussion, and the wind orchestra itself. His musical language was unique ... no other composer composed in his style. From the first performance of *Prague,* Mr. Husa was a national (and, international) celebrity. He appeared as guest conductor with university ensembles all over the country. *Music for Prague, 1968* was performed at one of the early conferences of the World Association for Symphonic Bands and Ensembles (WASBE) in Valencia, Spain . . . in the city's arena for bull fighting . . . in a midnight performance. It was estimated there were ten thousand people in the audience.

I was also present for his return to Prague in the spring of 1991. I was in Switzerland, as part of my first sabbatical. Mr. Husa had written to me, saying that he would be conducting a concert in Prague that spring. A good friend and I flew to Prague for the performance . . . it was in Smetana Hall, with the Czech Philharmonic. On the day of the concert, we went to the Hall to see about tickets. The ticket office was closed, and we could not determine what our course of action should be. Apparently, I knew that there was a rehearsal in the afternoon. So, we waited for the musicians to start arriving at the Hall . . . got in among a group of five or so of the musicians as they entered the building; began to talk nonchalantly as if we belonged there . . . and walked past the officials charged with keeping the public out. We found our way backstage, and met Karel. He was very happy to see me, and promised there would be tickets for me that evening. Of course, it was a spectacular performance!

Everyone who knew Mr. Husa has a story to tell about him. I would bet that all of them would speak to his gentle nature . . . his humility and generosity. I hosted a festival each year at Modesto College, and invited him to be the star attraction in 1977. We had invited several university bands, and one of them performed *Music for Prague*, with Karel conducting. He was magnificent . . . enormously expressive, quite animated. It was always a shock to see him go from the kind, gentle and serene soul that he was . . . to this inferno of energy and expression. Remarkable conductor! After one of the morning sessions . . . his piano music, I was trying to extricate him from the throngs of students and others who wanted to speak to him and be with him. I was trying to get him to lunch before another session in the afternoon, and kept saying, "we need to go; we really need to go." Finally, he looked at me and said quietly, "You go ahead, Ron . . . I need to be with these people. I'll be fine." He always had time

"Kindness is more important than wisdom, and the recognition of this is the beginning of wisdom."
     ~ Theodore Rubin ~

for young people . . . that was always the most important thing for him. That moment has stayed with me to this day.

In our many conversations at conferences and conventions, his visits to Modesto and to Cedar Falls (UNI), and the many phone conversations, Mr. Husa told me things about *Prague* and *Apotheosis* that I did not know . . . much of which I have not found in other sources. And, it seems appropriate that I should record those brief moments within this discussion. The first of these is in the second movement of *Prague*, the "Aria." He told me that he conceived this movement as a sort of "funeral march" . . . an idea which immediately changed my perception of the movement. He further noted that the sonorous tones in the opening twenty-five or so measures, played by the low brass, are intended to represent the deep bell sounds which he heard from the bell towers of Prague. When he said this to me, I could better understand those long "pedals" in context with the other "bell" sounds notated in the vibraphone and marimba. The sounds of bells are heard throughout the composition, as Prague is known as "The City of a Hundred Spires." These small revelations of what he was thinking, and hearing in his mind, completely transformed my understanding of this music.

He also revealed to me some of the circumstances of actually composing the piece. It seems that, during his tenure at Cornell University in Ithaca, New York, he had a "weekend cottage" in the small village of Interlaken, on Lake Cayuga, where he would spend his summers and weekends composing. It was there that he heard the BBC broadcast of the Soviet invasion of Prague on August 20, 1968. Around that same time, he had received a commission from Kenneth Snapp, at Ithaca College, to compose a piece for the Concert Band. Mr. Husa spent the next six weeks composing what would become his signature piece, *Music for Prague, 1968*. During this composing period, he would travel on Sunday evenings from Interlaken to the Howard Johnson's Motel on Route 13 north of Ithaca, where he would meet with Mr. Snapp and deliver the manuscript score of what he had composed in the previous week. They would drink a cup of coffee, and speak about the progress of

the work, and then Mr. Snapp would take that score to have parts
extracted for the players. On the final weekend, in which he was to
have the entire work completed, Mr. Husa discovered that he was
quickly getting to the end of his supply of score paper. The last two
pages of the printed score, the final eight measures from letter V to
the end, were written on his last sheet of manuscript paper. He sent
me a copy of that final page, which I attached to the back page of
my printed score. It is amazing how it changed my understanding
of this final section when I could see the entire eight measures as
a single idea, rather than what we see on the printed score of two
measures on the front of the page, and the final six on the back.

Another couple of small memories are about the *Apotheosis*. When
he came to the Northern Iowa campus in 1991, I picked him up at
the small airport in Waterloo/Cedar Falls. As we drove to campus,
he was quite excited to tell me a story about something that had
happened earlier that morning. He had stopped by his office at
Cornell to get something he needed for this trip, and when he arrived on campus, the place was filled with thousands of Canadian
geese, an unusual and extraordinary sight. It seems that the geese
were following their annual migration route to the South for the
winter, and had normally stopped off at Lake Cayuga for a rest. But,
the area around the lake and the town of Ithaca had experienced a
dense cloud cover for the past few days. So, while their internal nav-
igation system told the geese that there should be water somewhere
below, their vision was obscured and they could not see the lake.
They had missed it by about a mile!! Karel said that the geese were
walking around campus, making lots of noise, as if complaining,
"Where the heck is the lake?"

Some days before Karel's arrival, one of my neighbors had loaned
me a VHS recording of a short story involving a man who had
"parented" a group of hatchling geese, when their mother was
accidentally killed. The man also piloted an ultralight aircraft, and
the geese grew up learning to fly alongside their "mother" flying
the ultralight. That story eventually found its way to international
attention by way of YouTube, along with several similar stories. For
a memory of his time with us, I made a copy of that original video

and sent it to the Maestro. He was always so fascinated by anything concerned with our planet ... its forests, oceans, or wildlife. He was very happy to receive the recording, and wrote that he played it for several of his friends.

It was also during this 1991 visit that he told me something about the impetus, and inspiration, for his musical depiction of the destruction of Mother Earth. He said that he very often had dinner with another member of the Cornell faculty, the world-famous astrophysicist, Dr. Carl Sagan. He said that they often spoke about Sagan's studies of the universe, and also about the terrible state of affairs happening here on Planet Earth. From these dinner conversations, Karel imagined a scenario of what could happen in the future ... what an astronaut might observe in a return flight to Earth from somewhere in our galaxy. These imaginings coalesced into the program notes printed in the front of the score. He said that he had also been in contact with the legendary biologist and environmentalist, Dr. Roger Payne, who had completed his doctorate at Cornell, and was the first person to record whale songs. Payne apparently made those recordings available to several musicians and composers, including Mr. Husa. Alan Hovhaness, the great Armenian–American composer, used those recordings in his magnificent composition, *And God Created Great Whales*. In the second movement of *Apotheosis*, near the end, beginning at measure 132, Mr. Husa uses the horn section ... playing portamento "rips" ... to emulate the sounds of these whale songs. It is a chilling moment in the music!

There are a couple of videos which the reader may find helpful in discovering more of the spirit of this gifted composer and human being. The first is from a performance by the Illinois State University Wind Symphony of several of Karel's works at a special performance given during the 2005 Midwest Clinic in Chicago. Mr. Husa speaks of his impetus and inspiration for these works between each performance.[12]

The other video is from an interview believed to have been given prior to a performance of the orchestral version of *Music for Prague, 1968* by the North Carolina Symphony in January of 2011.[13]

[12] One can find this video at
https://youtu.be/w900rn2o9kA

[13] https://youtu.be/gdd_1vV2ftA

Mr. Husa had an enormous impact on my life, both personally and professionally. He shared many personal stories with me … of his life, and of his music. He helped me to imagine what he felt and thought as he was composing *Prague* and the *Apotheosis.* He was an inspiration for me, and I still miss him. Along with Kamilló and Frici Bacsí, he was like a father for me … what better models could one hope for?

> *"Listen to your life. See it for the fathomless mystery that it is …*
> *Touch, taste, smell your way to the holy and hidden part of it because,*
> *in the last analysis, all moments are key moments, And life itself is grace."*
> ~ Frederick Buechner ~

Programming

WITH REGARD TO PROGRAMMING, I developed a practice early on that helped to make the process a little easier. Concert scheduling occurred a year or two out, so we were always able to know performance dates at least a year before. Through the season, I collected "new" scores from a variety of sources ... scores that colleagues, in this country and others, told me about; scores that I learned about at conventions and conferences, and scores that composers would often send for perusal. I also set aside a stack of scores from the "core repertoire" that needed consideration for the coming year. For years, I had an actual list (about one hundred) of compositions which I included in my core repertoire, so I always consulted that to see what should be considered. By the end of the academic year, I usually had somewhere between sixty and seventy scores to think and feel about. After a couple of weeks of rest from the stress of the previous year, I began to look at the collected scores. I usually gave this about a month ... looking at a few scores each day, and sorting them into stacks of "yes," "maybe," and "no." I also looked at programs from the last few years to discover when was the last time a particular piece was performed.

Some years ago, I came to realize that the great majority of wind music was "program" music ... music written for a specific occasion, or inspired by a particular event or person. Husa's *Prague* and *Apotheosis* are examples of this. Eric Whitacre's *October*; Steven Bryant's *Alchemy in Silent Spaces*, and Jerome Sorcsek's *Portrait of Faustus* are also good examples. In program music, the composer

"I am an artist ... it's self-evident that what that word implies is looking for something all the time without ever finding it in full. It is the opposite of saying, 'I know all about it. I've already found it.' As far as I'm concerned, the word means, 'I am looking. I am hunting for it, I am deeply involved.'

~ Vincent Van Gogh ~

attempts to "tell a story" about a specific event or person. Or, per-haps, the composer is inspired by a particular person or event, and attempts to capture the emotions of that moment. This concept of program music started in the nineteenth century with composers such as Hector Berlioz, Richard Strauss, Bedřich Smetana, and others. While program music is certainly a legitimate style of com-position, and the concept has produced numerous masterpieces, it suffers from one distinctive feature ... it attempts to direct the emotions of the listener. Husa's *Apotheosis* focuses the attention of the listener on the destruction of the earth ... not a happy thought! Again, directing the emotions of the listener is not, in and of itself, a bad idea or one without merit.

My reservation here is that the overwhelming preponderance of compositions for wind orchestra ... especially those composed in the last twenty-five years or so ... were composed as *program music.* Noticeably absent from the wind repertoire is what we call *absolute music* ... music composed *without* programmatic reference. A symphony from Beethoven, or a concerto from Tchaikovsky, or a suite by Bartók does not intend to call forth a specific emotion, or set of emotions, from the listener. The listener is free to be inspired and moved by the music itself; independent of programmatic content. Thus, it was part of my intention, in programming, to find and include symphonies, concerti, divertimenti, suites ... and other compositions of a non-programmatic nature. Thus, the *Divertimento for Band* from Vincent Persichetti; the Hindemith *Symphony in B-flat*; David Gillingham's *Concertino for Four Percussion and Wind Orchestra*, and Arnold Schönberg's *Theme and Variations,* op. 43A.

And, I wanted our students to have direct experience with musical forms. They learn about forms in history classes, analyze forms in theory classes ... it seems logical that they should also know about forms from an experiential perspective ... performing them. So, I wanted to include works that used traditional forms ... sonata, theme and variations, rondo, and others.

I also wanted them to have experience with ensembles and soloists not normally associated with wind groups ... choruses, singers, string soloists, pianists, etc. Thus, my request from Maestro Hidas for his *Requiem*, for SATB chorus; SATB soloists, and wind orchestra. We also performed the magnificent *Requiem*, op. 70 of German composer, Rolf Rudin . . . and the world premiere of his *Te Deum*, op. 93 for male chorus and wind orchestra. We programmed works with solo voices . . . soprano, alto, tenor, and bass, both original and transcribed. There were pieces for piano soloist, as well as solo violin and solo cello. And, of course, we had works for all the traditional wind soloists . . . flute, oboe, bassoon, clarinet, saxophone, horn, trumpet, trombone, euphonium, tuba, and percussion.

It is my belief that students should sing as much as possible. In singing, our bodies become our instrument, and we feel more "in tune" with the music; its resonance and vibrations. So, we performed Ron Nelson's *Medieval Suite* several times; Dan Bukvich's *Agincourt Hymn* and *The Dream of Abraham*, and Yasuhide Ito's *Glorioso*.

In the last fifteen to twenty years, maybe longer, there has been a trend toward shorter pieces in the band/wind ensemble world . . . somewhere between five and eight minutes. It is my belief that audiences need some time to engage the music; to become conscious of the aural motion seeking to engage the emotions of the listener. As most people are visually "dominant," it is important that we do what we can to minimize those things which take the listener away from the music itself. That's one of the reasons that professional players wear black concert dress . . . to minimize the visual effect on the audience. The lights in the concert hall are focused on the players . . . it is dark in the audience. We request that people turn off cell phones and pagers, and that they not take photos during the performance. All of this is in an effort to make it easier for the audience to give their attention to the aural sensations of the music itself . . . not to the attendant visual elements. But, even with all that, it still takes time for the listener to engage with the music. So, with these shorter pieces, they are often concluded before the listener can be completely focused on listening. While there are certainly many excellent compositions that are only a few minutes

"It takes a very long time to become young.
~ Pablo Picasso ~

in length, I believe it important that the great majority of the program be comprised of pieces longer in length. So, I looked for works between fifteen and thirty minutes in length. The Requiems of Mr. Hidas and Mr. Rudin are right around an hour in duration. As noted earlier, when programming music of Percy Grainger, I would take three or four shorter pieces of four or five minutes, and set them together as a "suite," thereby creating a longer, more satisfying musical experience. Generally, I looked to program four to six pieces for each concert . . . thirty-five to forty minutes of music for each half.

In summary, with regard to programming, I was guided by consideration of core repertoire; chamber music, and newly composed works. I also wanted to have a balance of programmatic works and absolute music. I believed it important that students have direct (performing) experience with the traditional genres and forms of music. And, I wanted them to have experiences with other musical instruments and ensembles . . . choruses, string players, pianists, and singers. I also believed it important to program more substantive pieces, in terms of length.

So, with the sixty or so scores that I collected each year, and sorted into "yes," "no," and "maybe" piles, I began to put together programs for the coming year. In addition to considerations already mentioned, there were a couple of other factors that were considered. The Scholarship Benefit Concert, the "magnum opus" for the School of Music each year, was usually scheduled in the last week of September. Thus, if the Wind Symphony was to have a major role in that production, that had to be factored into the planning. Each spring, we held the Wind Symphony Solo Competition for our students, with the winner being scheduled for the following fall. Normally, I wanted to have at least one soloist each season, usually one of our artist faculty. And, if it was a "tour year" for the Wind Symphony, that was a major factor in choosing repertoire.

Usually, I was able to finalize repertoire for the season by early July, giving me the remainder of the summer for initial score study. Ensemble auditions occurred in the few days before the fall semester began, so I posted the season's repertoire on the call board

"What is meant by the term 'illusion' is that phenomena do not exist independently of other phenomena; that their appearance of independent existence is illusory. This is all that is meant by 'illusion,' not that something is not really there.
~ HH The Dalai Lama ~

outside the rehearsal room for all to see. I found that informing the students of what was coming for the season helped them to better understand what was needed from them, and to incorporate concert dates into their semester's schedule.

Now that the repertoire was known, it became important to plan a rehearsal schedule that would allow for proper preparation of the programs. I noted the number of rehearsals available for each program, and the number of hours contained therein. Next, I would apportion those hours among the compositions scheduled for performance ... some pieces getting more time; others less. The Hindemith *Symphony*, for instance, usually required more rehearsal time than a trio of pieces from Percy Grainger. Then, I would schedule the hours allotted for each piece throughout the weeks available. I laid all this out on a grid ... indicating rehearsal dates, and amount of rehearsal time for each composition. This was only for me ... so that I had a mental image of how rehearsals should progress. As the rehearsal process started, I was able to adjust the rehearsal times as needed ... this piece was going better than anticipated, and required less time ... that piece was more difficult than anticipated, and needed some more time. Each Friday, I published the rehearsal schedule for the next week, and posted it on the call board outside the rehearsal hall. As technology progressed, and electronic mail (e-mail) became available, I also sent the schedule to all the players. This allowed the players to plan for the following week, and prepare appropriately. If there were players not needed for a particular piece, they could plan on using that time for study or practice.

As most of our players were music majors, and had already played their instrument at some point before rehearsal, it was not so necessary to do "warm-ups" at the beginning of rehearsal. What was necessary was a means to get their minds and spirits "in the room" as quickly as possible. Derived from Eastern meditation techniques, we developed a vocalizing/breathing technique consist-ing of singing vowels at pitches that allowed for free vibration in the cranial cavity; the chest, and the abdomen. In effect, we were massaging the central nervous system. This was quite successful, as it allowed the players (and, myself) to calm the mind rather quickly, and start to bring our focus into the room. That took about five minutes. Students reported that they also found this technique helpful in their individual practice sessions. After this, we would usually rehearse one of four or five works we kept in the folders as part of our "rehearsal repertoire" noted above.

Development

IN THINKING THROUGH OUR HISTORY, and noticing the different changes and transformations that occurred through those thirty-five years, I believe that our development can be organized into three separate, but connected, periods. They are as follows:

I. 1982–1991

The beginning of my tenure at Northern Iowa until my first sabbatical in the spring of 1991. We made a name change, from "Wind Ensemble" to "Wind Symphony" and, in accordance with that, made substantive changes to the mission of the group. We also changed the name, and conception, of the Tallcorn Band Festival to the Northern Festival of Bands. And, the ensemble began to develop its identity and reputation in the state of Iowa, and those surrounding.

II. 1991–2000

We started to tour internationally ... three tours to Hungary in this period. We experienced an expansion of performance repertoire, owing to my travels in Europe, as well as other sources, and we started to produce compact disc recordings. We moved into the new Performing Arts Center the spring of 2000 ... a major nexus in our development.

III. 2000–2017

In this final period, we made three concert tours in Italy; started to produce video productions for posting on YouTube, and expanded, again, our performing possibilities. This period includes my second sabbatical in the spring of 2001, my Fulbright year in Hungary during the 2004–2005 academic year; the developing relationships with composers; the addition of the Northern Iowa Band Invitational, and the creation of the Iowa Band Conductors Forum.

I. 1982–1991

MUCH HAS ALREADY BEEN WRITTEN about those first couple of years. It was a time of building and establishing a foundation for continuing growth. All of the new practices, introduced in that first year, continued to become part of our heritage and traditions. Rehearsals were in Room 60, in the basement of Russell Hall, home for the School of Music. When Russell Hall opened in 1962, it was considered a state-of-the-art facility. But, the passage of time revealed a few design flaws in certain areas. Room 60 was the primary rehearsal space for the instrumental ensembles, and was built with tiered, semi-circular seating for players ... making alternative seating arrangements virtually impossible. This problem was further confounded by the fact that we were not able to perform with tiered seating in the Russell Hall Auditorium, presently known as Bengtson Auditorium. It was also quite difficult to find time in the auditorium for rehearsals, as this was also the primary practice facility for the organ students. The organ professor at that time protected the space as a mother bear protects her cubs. While I understood and sympathized with the need for practice space and time for organ students, I did not believe that the needs of the ensembles should be sacrificed for the needs of a relatively few students. That was an ongoing discussion!

I did everything I could think of to help the sound in that performance space. We used reflecting shells in as many configurations as

possible ... some worked; most did not. There was a deep orchestra
pit for stage productions ... making it somewhat dangerous to get
too close to the edge of the stage. Everything had to be transported
from Room 60 up to the stage by way of an elevator ... chairs,
stands, percussion equipment, all of it. Doing this in the ten minutes allotted before rehearsals was an ordeal, to say the least. And,
when the rehearsal was finished, we had to load up everything
and take it back down to Room 60. We did this for almost twenty
years ... until we moved to the new facility, the Gallagher-Bluedorn
Performing Arts Center (PAC) in the spring of 2000.

Perhaps the most substantive change in this early period was the
restructuring of our annual band festival for high school students,
the Tallcorn Band Festival. This was the oldest continuous university sponsored band festival for high school students in the state
of Iowa, beginning in 1953. During the first couple of years, as I
was visiting high schools around the state and gathering the band
directors' perceptions of what we were doing in the School of Music,
I learned that they were not particularly enthusiastic about our
event. The teachers told me that there was little which set our event
apart from the other similar festivals around the state. The reader
should know that almost every university and college in the state
has a band festival of some sort ... certainly, the "Big 5": University
of Northern Iowa, Iowa State University, University of Iowa, Drake
University, and Luther College. Several of the smaller schools also
had similar events. There were also the six District honor bands
of the Iowa Bandmasters Association. And, there were conference
honor bands ... a group of schools whose athletic teams competed
with each other. All told, I would imagine there were thirty to forty
honor bands in the state, of one sort or another.

For the years prior to my arrival, and the first two or three after I
arrived, the event was a two-day affair ... always the second full
weekend in February. There were two bands of about one hundred
players each; one for 9th and 10th grade students (Blue Band), and
the other for 11th and 12th grade students (Gold Band). The students
arrived on Friday afternoon, were auditioned for chair placement,
and began rehearsals. The Wind Symphony performed a concert

*"Life is what happens to us while we are making
other plans."*
~ Thomas Le Mance ~

in the evening. Saturday was given to more rehearsals, along with auditions for the Solo Competition, open to all students invited to the festival. The final concert, featuring both bands and the student solo winner, was held at 8:00 PM on Saturday evening.

After a few years of this, we started to consider some changes which I felt were needed. I believed that the reason for an event such as this had been lost over the years. As there were now many such events around the state, it seemed there was nothing unique about what we were offering. I envisioned an event in which it would be possible to offer the students, and their teachers, a wider range of learning opportunities, something more than "just playing in another honor band." So, in 1988, we transformed the festival, and renamed it the Northern Festival of Bands. Now, it started on Thursday afternoon with the final concert slated for Saturday afternoon. We added an elegant banquet on Saturday noon for all the participants in the Commons Ballroom on campus. That was something none of the other festivals had. We decreased the number of students invited, so that the two bands were now between seventy-five and eighty players; a bit more manageable. Fewer students increased the quality of the ensembles significantly. We renamed the bands . . . Concert Band (grades 9–10) and Symphony Band (grades 11–12). We began offering a substantial scholarship to the winner of the Solo Competition, contingent on the student being admitted to UNI, and choosing music as a major.

The music faculty became more involved in the event, presenting master classes for each instrument. We offered sessions for the teachers . . . repertoire; pedagogy; round-table discussions, and many others. We added "Lobby Concerts" to the schedule . . . short twelve- to fifteen-minute concerts in the lobby between festival events. The most popular ensembles were the Percussion groups (Taiko or West African Drumming), the Tuba-Euphonium Ensemble, the Flute Choir, and other chamber ensembles (both students and faculty). As thing progressed, we included other ensembles: saxophones, trombones, and occasionally a double reed group. We added the Symphonic Band on the Friday evening performance, sharing it with the Wind Symphony. And, beginning in 1992, we began inviting conductors from other countries to come and make music with the students.

Over the years, we brought an impressive array of world class conductors to the plains of Iowa. Among them were Felix Hauswirth (Switzerland), László Marosi (Hungary), Rafi Primo (Israel), John Bourgeois (Conductor, United States Marine Band), Janis Purins (Latvia), Lewis Buckley (Conductor, United States Coast Guard Band), Lorenzo Della Fonte (Italy), Bert Aalders (Netherlands), and Denis Salvini (Italy).

We also began to make more, and better, use of our students in managing the festival. The band fraternity, Kappa Kappa Psi, was available to help with logistics for the final Saturday concert. We assigned a senior level, or graduate, student to each band to serve as a sort of "manager." Their task was to take care of the students in each band, get them from one rehearsal space to the next; help with occasional instrument repair needs, gather the folders after each rehearsal and distribute at the next, and take care of whatever the guest conductor might need. I learned a lot about our students during these events . . . how responsible they could be, and how interested they were in being involved. As our university students were not much older than the high school students, it allowed our high school guests to better imagine themselves as a future student at UNI. And, it was an opportunity for our students to know aspects of their future profession which can only be learned experientially, not from lectures or books.

I remember one particular year, during the final concert. It was during the "change-over" from the Concert Band to the Symphony Band. The student manager for the Symphony Band went on to the stage and began to move chairs and stands; making the necessary changes before the high school students came on stage. I wandered out onto the stage, and also began moving chairs and stands . . . thinking I also knew where things should go. The young woman looked at me, and, in a commanding voice, said, "Do you want me to do this, or do you want to do it?" I responded: "You!" She continued, "I have a plan for this; I know what I'm doing, and you're interfering!" I held up my hands, made a gesture of apology, and left the stage.

From that moment forward, I always allowed the students to decide how best to handle the tasks assigned to them. I would ask them to my office, offer them the assignment, and tell them that they should decide the best way to accomplish the intended goals. I said something like, "You decide what to do, and get whomever you need to help you. If a problem comes up, you solve it. I will support whatever choices and decisions you make during the weekend. If you choose wrongly, we will have a discussion on Monday. But, for the weekend, this is your job . . . you get to decide how to do it." I was never disappointed . . . they always handled their assignments with efficiency and professionalism. The only problems arose when someone outside the chain of command . . . perhaps, another faculty member . . . interfered with the student's plan. That only happened a couple of times, and in both cases, the student was correct with her plan.

"Every thing has its rightful place. And, in its rightful place . . . it becomes beautiful."
~ Grey Owl ~

We accomplished our goal; the changes made an immediate difference to the quality and appeal of the festival. We started attracting a better quality student to the event and, subsequently, to the university. We took a short poll one year, asking our wind and percussion students what things were considered when deciding where to attend college. A little more than 90% indicated that they had attended the Northern Festival, and were impressed with our facilities, our ensembles, and our faculty. Over the years, the festival continued to evolve, making small improvements when necessary. Of course, circumstances have changed dramatically since the late 1980s. Indeed, the whole world is different from what it was in the days before cell phones, computers, and round-the-clock television.

The school music programs in the state have not been immune to those changes. Each year, as we began planning for the festival and discussing whatever changes were needed, we endeavored always to be guided in our decisions by what would be best for the students and teachers we invited to our campus. We wanted the repertoire that they studied and performed to be substantive and of a higher quality than they might be able to perform in their own school ensembles. By way of our guest conductors, we were able to offer the students experiences with music and traditions from other countries; music that they otherwise might never know. With our ensembles and faculty, we hoped to inspire the students to a higher level of expectation for their own abilities. In short, we wanted—as a consequence of the students being with us for the three days of the festival—to help them be better musicians when they returned home; to inspire them to always have music in their lives.

Our increased focus on recruiting more, and better prepared, students to the School of Music began to find traction. In the mid-1980s, in consultation with the Director and other members of the faculty, we launched an entirely new array of printed materials for recruitment purposes. And, we began a "team" approach to recruiting ... sending one of our faculty chamber ensembles to perform and work with students in the high schools. We started to formulate lists of potential students, and communicate with them on a regular basis. All of these efforts started to pay dividends rather quickly, and the quality of incoming freshmen increased significantly. This, of course, had a positive effect on the Wind Symphony.

THE WIND SYMPHONY began to find its identity in this period. The new practices and expectations[14], which initially caused concern among many of the players, started to become more comfortable. These practices were integrated into our rehearsals and performances, and, in a few years, the students no longer remembered a time when these customs were not part of our heritage and culture.

[14] Noted earlier, pp. 38–44

We performed, a couple of times, at the annual gathering of the Iowa Bandmasters Association, and continued the previous practice of short, two- to three-day tours to perform in high schools in Iowa and surrounding states.

The Chamber Wind Players was formed during this time, and was an immediate boost to the program. Chamber music ... both rehearsing and performing ... makes players better. It just does. There are many books that will give the reader data as to why chamber music is good for musicians. There are other books to inform one about the history of the various chamber ensembles, and still others with information about ways to form chamber ensembles in school settings; how to integrate chamber music into the curriculum. But for me, it was pretty simple . . . the players *liked it!* Students enjoy making music in small groups. The music is often more substantive, and challenging to each individual player. They find it easier to develop listening and intonation skills in small groups. And, for us, it was a perfect means with which to commune with composers from earlier historical periods . . . Mozart, Haydn, Beethoven, Dvorák, etc. Of course, as I indicated in an earlier section[15], music from earlier periods does not exist for all instruments . . . notably low brass, saxophones, and percussion. But, there is plenty of chamber music for those instruments in the twentieth century. And, the skills that we learned with chamber music transferred quite nicely into the larger ensembles . . . the Wind Symphony and Symphony Orchestra. I believe that the creation of the Chamber Wind Players was the single best reason that we were able to make great strides with the Wind Symphony. And, again, the students loved it!

[15] See pp. 47–49

II. 1991–2000

MY FIRST SABBATICAL was in the spring semester of 1991. My project was to travel in Europe and learn as much as possible about wind music from that part of the world. My good friend and colleague, Felix Hauswirth, graciously invited me to be a guest in his home in Zug, Switzerland, for that spring. Felix was, and is, one of the more important leaders of the profession, and was enormously supportive in helping me to gain a better understanding of the areas of significant composers and performing ensembles in Europe. Felix was quite sympathetic of my interests and invited me to work with his ensemble, the Stadtmusik Zug. He also invited me to serve as guest conductor for the Schweizer Jugend Blasorchester (Swiss National Youth Wind Orchestra) for its annual gathering of

"Computers are useless. They can only give you answers."

~ Pablo Picasso ~

rehearsals and concerts. And, he generously invited me to share in several conducting workshops in Germany and Austria. These occasions were a great experience for me, as they allowed me to better understand the heritage and traditions of wind music in those countries.

This was also the occasion of my first trip to Hungary. Some weeks before my departure from Cedar Falls, Maestro Whitwell phoned and told me that he had recently returned from a trip to Italy, where he had been a member of the jury for a performance competition … mostly singers and pianists. Also on the jury was Árpád Balázs, who was, at that time, President of the Hungarian Band Association. I learned later that he was also an accomplished composer, composing works for the wind orchestra, as well as music for chorus, strings, and ballets. David sent me his business card, which had a mailing address indicated. I wrote a letter (once more, the reader will please recall a time before the internet and email), indicating my interest in learning more about Hungarian wind music, and asking if it might be possible for me to come for a visit. I did not hear back from him before leaving for Switzerland, but some weeks after my arrival, his kind response and invitation was forwarded to me at Felix's address in Zug. He did not speak or write English, but his son, Ádám, was quite proficient in both writing and speaking English. So, by phone, I arranged for a week's visit, around the beginning of May.

I took an early morning train from Zug to Budapest, arriving around 10:00 PM in the evening, at the West (Nyugati) train station. My hosts, Maestro Balázs and son, Ádám, met me at the station with flowers and champagne. I wish that I had been alert enough to recognize their courtesy and goodwill as only the "tip of the iceberg" for what was to come. They took me to my hotel for the week … a lovely boutique hotel on the Buda side, overlooking the Danube. My initiation into Hungarian culture began in earnest the next morning around 9:00 AM. Unfortunately, I did not write down all of the events, or their sequence, that happened that week … as was to become my practice later. So, I am not sure exactly where and with whom was the first appointment. What

"The world is full of obvious things which nobody by any chance ever observes."
~ Arthur Conan Doyle ~

I *do* remember was that everyone was quite well dressed ... suit or sport coat with long tie for the men and dresses below the knee for women was *de rigueur* at that time. In every occasion that week, this was the dress for Hungarians. Luckily, I had brought along appropriate attire. Anyway, that first morning meeting began with formal introductions and handshakes. Immediately afterward, a woman brought a tray of small glasses, filled with some unknown liquid, into the center of the gathering. Each person took a glass and waited for our host to, again, formally welcome me to Hungary. Then, each person drank the contents of their glass in one gulp, followed by the customary, *jó* ... good! It was my first encounter with the national drink of Hungary ... *palinka!* I was to have repeated encounters with this amazing liquid throughout the week!

It was during my first visit that I met almost all of the important Hungarian (living) composers. My hosts were so kind to immerse me in the Hungarian musical life ... long days and short nights! I met Messers Hidas and Lendvay, as well as several other lesser known composers. I was taken to a rehearsal of the Central Band of the Hungarian Army—an ensemble akin to one of the top service bands in Washington—where I met László Marosi for the first time. László's English was excellent, and we were together several times during that trip. When I was first introduced to him, he said something like, "Oh yes, I know who you are!" When I asked how this was, he replied, "Jim Croft was here recently, and he brought me your album, *Rainbow Gardens*." James Croft, very well known in the profession, was Director of Bands at Florida State University from 1981 until 2003. He had completed his Master's degree at Northern Iowa back in the early 1950s, when it was known as Iowa State Teacher's College. The *Rainbow Gardens* recording was our first public release, offered in cassette form in the fall of 1990. I had sent a copy to Dr. Croft, who apparently took it along for his visit in Hungary that spring.

I was also taken to a rehearsal of the Hungarian National Philharmonic for a rehearsal of a Mahler symphony. I was invited to sit in the violin section, near the back, where I could soak up the sounds of this fabulous orchestra. It was a wonderful experience! Maestro Balázs took me to a music store in Budapest where I could buy music for wind orchestra. I found several pieces from both Frici and Kamilló, as well as several other lesser known composers. At that time, score and parts for a complete work were about $2.00 in American currency. This was 1991, and Hungary was only just beginning to awaken from the Communist period, a period of which several of my new friends referred to as "The Big Sleep." During this period, composers worked for the state, and composed music primarily to be performed by musicians and ensembles in Hungary. Prices for everything were tightly controlled, and money was scarce. So, prices for everything were incredibly low, compared to Western standards. As luggage space was limited, I only bought a few pieces in my first visit. But, the following year, my second visit, I think I bought all the remaining available works . . . though the prices had increased by then, but not much!

All in all, my first visit to Hungary was the beginning of a beautiful relationship . . . one that would lead to many more visits, including three concert tours with the Wind Symphony. I was invited back the next year (March 1992) to conduct concerts with the Wind Orchestra of the Hungarian Customs Administration . . . a professional ensemble with regular rehearsals and a busy performance schedule. Following that, I returned every year, sometimes twice a year, for many years. On a couple of occasions, I was a guest of the Hungarian Army Music School. I presented several conducting workshops, with the assistance of Maestro Marosi, and was guest conductor with both professional and municipal ensembles. I returned for more study again in 2001, as part of my second sabbatical, and was awarded a Fulbright Senior Lecturer Grant at the Pécsi Tudományegyetem (University of Pécs) for the 2004–2005 academic year.

That 1991 sabbatical trip was a major turning point in both my career, and the direction of the Wind Symphony. I found new sources for excellent wind music from composers in Hungary, Germany, Switzerland, and Austria. More importantly, I was connected to a new arena of musical activity. The people I met, and the relationships I established, were to become a plentiful source for music, and other professional activity in the coming years. I discovered excellent conductors, several of whom I was able to bring to Iowa to appear as guest conductor for the Northern Festival of Bands.

For the next ten years, I was in Hungary every year. We took the Wind Symphony there for its first tour outside the USA in March of 1993 . . . sponsored by the Hungarian Customs Administration. We returned again in 1996, sponsored by the Hungarian Wind Music Association, and the final Hungarian tour was in March of 2000.[16] These experiences helped us to discover more of our abilities and honed our performing skills. Playing five or so performances in a week, of the same repertoire, was helpful in developing confidence. And, performing before wildly enthusiastic audiences at every occasion helped us to develop a bit of "swagger" . . . which, again, fed into the confidence of the players. Between tours, the stories that the players told their friends and families . . . and their high school band directors, and friends at other universities . . . these helped to raise the profile of the group . . . we were working our way toward "legend." At that time, we were the only public university in the northern Midwest taking regular concert tours in Europe. This became a great factor in recruiting.

As a consequence of that 1991 sabbatical, and my new-found relationships with European musicians and composers, we were able to bring several of them to Iowa to work with the high school students in the Northern Festival of Bands, as well as our university students in the Wind Symphony. This, too, helped the students to feel more confident and connected to the larger world of music. As noted earlier, Mr. Hidas composed a piece especially for us after our '93 tour (*Almost B.A.C.H.*). Mr. Lendvay came in the spring of 1994 for the American premiere of his *Concerto for Trumpet*, with Randy Grabowski as soloist. László Marosi from Hungary, Janis Purins, conductor from Latvia, and Lorenzo Della Fonte from Italy, came and worked with the group, as well as several other Europeans.

[16] The reader will find a more complete account of these adventures under the section, Concert Tours.

"Absence of evidence is not evidence of absence."
~ Martin Rees ~

IT WAS DURING this second period that the Wind Symphony recorded four albums: *Rainbow Gardens* (1990), *Memories* (1994), *Genesis* (1995), and *Requiem* (1997).[17] The first was issued in cassette form; the other three as compact discs. I think we made five hundred copies of each recording. I only have a few of the *Memories* disc left, and none of the other three. So, they must have sold fairly well. The only other recording we made, *The Best of All Possible Worlds*, was in 2004, after our first tour in Italy.

In the spring (April) of 2000, we moved into our new facility, the Gallagher-Bluedorn Performing Arts Center. Without making any other structural changes, the Wind Symphony improved dramatically ... simply by performing in this wonderful space, the Great Hall. While we all knew that a world-class performance venue would greatly enhance everything that we did, we were truly impressed by how much better our music making sounded in this amazing new place. Now, the players could hear each other much easier, within sections and across sections. And, from the audience perspective, one could hear everything now, regardless of where one sat. It was a remarkable difference!

[17] For a complete list of compositions on each album, the reader may refer to the appendix.

"Don't play what's there; play what's not there."
~ Miles Davis ~

Figure 11: The Great Hall of the Gallagher-Bluedorn Performing Arts Center, University of Northern Iowa

The new rehearsal facility, Davis Hall, was also a great addition. Now, we had a flat surface, with a wooden floor, on which to rehearse. We could seat the ensemble in whatever configuration we chose ... and, replicate that arrangement in the Great Hall across the way. The acoustics in Davis Hall are very close to those in the Great Hall. So, what we rehearsed in Davis was virtually the same as what we heard in the Great Hall. This, again, was a dramatic lift for the Wind Symphony ... indeed, all of the ensembles in the School of Music.

Figure 12: Davis Hall, the rehearsal space in the Gallagher-Bluedorn Performing Arts Center, University of Northern Iowa

III. 2000–2017

IN THE SPRING SEMESTER OF 2001, I was given my second (and, final) sabbatical leave from the university. This project was quite similar to the one in 1991, but now on a much expanded scale, with experiences in many more countries. My friend, Felix Hauswirth, again invited me to use his home in Switzerland as a "home base" for my travels around Europe. I was invited as guest conductor with both professional and amateur ensembles in Germany, Latvia,

Sweden, Italy, Hungary, Slovenia, and Israel. I also had professional and tourist excursions in Vienna, the Czech Republic, and Poland.

This trip was my first occasion for a visit to Italy. Lorenzo Della Fonte, composer and conductor of the Orchestra di Fiati della Valtellina, invited me to serve as the "master teacher" for the final week of a conductor training course which he taught each year. The course had fifteen or so young conductors working with a live ensemble. I was able to work with them on score study and technical skills, with a concluding concert that included the awarding of a course diploma for each of the participants. It was an exceptionally fine visit; I was treated like royalty. This was the first of many visits to Italy . . . I returned on several occasions for more teaching and guest conducting. We took the Wind Symphony for concert tours in 2004, 2012, and finally in 2016. We were exceptionally well received in each visit, with capacity audiences at each concert. For many musicians in the northern part of Italy, the University of Northern Iowa was like the center of the universe![18]

[18] There will be further discussion of these tours under the section, Concert Tours.

THIS PERIOD ALSO INCLUDED the occasion for my second, and final, trip to Israel. My good friends, Rafi Primo and Joseph Hartmann, invited me for a week of teaching and conducting. The Israeli music programs are quite similar to the European model. Each village has a "music school" which is funded by the municipal administration. Here, there are teachers for each instrument, and ensembles which include a band, often an orchestra, and usually a chorus. In my visit, I was able to work with several youth bands, and was on the jury for a band competition . . . one similar to those found in America. I also met several Israeli composers, and was able to secure score and parts for several fine compositions to be performed later by the Wind Symphony. Among these works were Paul Ben-Chaim's *Fanfare to Israel*, Shimon Cohen's *Fantasia on a Yemenite Traditional Song*, Boris Pigovat's *Masada* (American Premiere), and Benjamin Yusopov's *Suite for Wind Orchestra*.

My two visits to Israel are among my most treasured of memories. The Israeli people are warm and inviting; very hospitable and engaging. My friends took me from the top of Israel . . . Metullah,

Figure 13: Frigyes Hidas, Ronald Johnson and Joseph Hartmann at Lake Balaton, Hungary

the Golan Heights, and the Galil (Sea of Galilee) . . . to the bottom . . . the Dead Sea, Ein Gedi, and Eilat, on the Red Sea. They also took me to Yad Vashem, the Holocaust Memorial in Jerusalem . . . an experience so profound that, on several occasions, I just sat down on a bench and wept. Israel is an amazing country, with wonderful people. There was a memorable moment during my first visit in 1997, when I was invited to a gala party celebrating the anniversary of the founding of the state of Israel . . . it was also the occasion of my birthday. At one point, I was called to the front of the room, where the people sang "Happy Birthday," and gave me several gifts, including a bottle of Israeli wine, marking the occasion. With calls of "speech, speech," I thanked my friends for their courtesy and kindness, and remarked that it was an amazing feeling to be older than a country . . . Israel was 49; I was 52!

It is one of my disappointments that I was not able to take the Wind Symphony there for a concert tour, though I considered it each time that it was our year for traveling. While I believe the state of Israel to be more safe and secure than the city of Chicago, I always worried that there would be some sort of tragic incident just before our departure . . . with the resultant fear from parents and students being enough to cancel our trip. Still, it would have been the most unforgettable trip we could have made.

IN MARCH OF 2002, in a beautiful ceremony in Vatican City (Rome), for "significant contributions to humanity," I was invested in L'Ordre des Chevaliers du Sinai (The Religious and Military Order of the Knights of St. Catherine of Sinai). The Order was founded in 737 AD, and counts among its members, Napoleon Bonaparte and Eleanor Roosevelt. The Order is closely associated with both the Knights of Malta and the Knights Templar. I had been nominated by my friend and mentor, David Whitwell, who had been invested in the Ordre Souverain et Militaire du Temple de Jerusalem in 1991.

Figure 14: Ceremony of Investiture

The first evening, in the Chiesa San Lorenzo, was given to the "Ceremony of the Vigil," a lovely ceremony in which the postulants are instructed in the duties of a Knight, and invited to reflect on the meaning of Chivalry. The following evening, the "Ceremony of Investiture," was held in the Chiesa Sant' Onofrio. We entered the church accompanied by "The Pilgrim's Chorus" from Wagner's opera about knighthood, *Tannhäuser*. Among the nine Chevaliers and four Dames invested in the Order that evening, there were two Brigadier Generals from the American Military, a gentleman from one of the royal families of Poland, myself, and others from Italy, England, and Canada. It was another beautiful ceremony, followed by an excellent meal at a lovely restaurant in the famous Piazza di Spagna. While this event was not directly related to my professional work, it most certainly was because of my work that the invitation to join the Order was extended. It was a great honor for me, and I have held to the values and ideals of Knighthood since that time.

DURING THE 2004–2005 ACADEMIC YEAR, I lived in Pécs, Hungary, as a Fulbright Senior Lecturer at the Pécsi Tudományegyetem (University of Pécs). Pécs is a beautiful city of around 150,000 people in the south of Hungary, about twenty miles from the Croatian border. The university was founded in 1367, one of the oldest universities in Europe. As noted earlier, I had been a yearly visitor to Hungary since 1991, and had established a good working relationship with several of the music faculty at the university. The Wind Symphony had been in Hungary for concerts in 1993, 1996, and 2000, and was well known among Hungary's bands … both amateur and professional. The primary thrust of the Fulbright Award was to assist in the creation of an international conducting program … something akin to a Master's level conducting program in America. And, I was to help in the process of aligning the practices of the university with those outlined in the Bologna Agreement of 1999. This was an attempt by the European Union to bring uniformity and standardization to European Higher Education. Among other things, I was asked to help them better understand the traditions and practices of American universities.

For instance, no one had the slightest idea of the process by which the number of credits was assigned to a particular course … what is the difference between a one credit course and a three credit course? Previous practice, common in most of Europe, was to have a single exam at the end of the course … a single individual sitting in front of the assembled faculty, and questioned about the semester's work. My efforts at periodic exams throughout the semester were *not* a lasting success! And, most interesting to me, were my efforts to help the music faculty to create and work with a "master calendar," one indicating all classes and other scheduled events. Previously, each member of the faculty was discrete . . . that is, they scheduled events for their students independently of consultation with other faculty. They could not understand why anyone else would be the least interested in what they were doing. It took a while to show them the advantages of a "team" effort, one where everyone was aware of what the others were doing.

Between the time of my application for the Fulbright program, and the actual notification of the award (and subsequent beginning of my tenure there) was about two years. This was enough time for economic conditions to change, yet again, in Hungary. While Hungary had certainly been one of the more open and progressive countries in the Communist era, she nonetheless had many obstacles to overcome in her quest to become a respected member of the world community. The national economy was, and still is, one of the larger issues. So, by the time of my arrival, the idea of an international conducting program had been reduced to one of a more regional nature.

The conducting curriculum was a two-year program, consisting of wind music history; score reading (transposing orchestral scores at the piano); arranging, and technical skills. These courses were divided among four faculty . . . I was given the task of teaching technical skills (baton technique). The students in the program had already completed their undergraduate diploma, and were teaching in a municipal music school in the region around Pécs.

Before I left Iowa, I was able to ship two medium sized boxes of books and audio recordings by way of the State Department's courier service. These were added to the library's collection in the Pécsi Tudományegyetem School of Music, and included books from David Whitwell, who is considered the "godfather" of research into the history of wind music in Western culture. At that time, there were no books printed in Hungary which focused on that area of music history. The recordings included an assortment of American university bands and ensembles, the military bands in Washington, D.C., and a few recordings by professional ensembles . . . especially wind chamber music. Recordings and books such as these were difficult to find in Hungary, and even had they been available for purchase, the necessary funds for such acquisitions would not have been sufficient. So, this collection was a great addition to the library resources of the School of Music.

The School of Music assigned a member of the piano faculty, András Körtesi, to be my assistant and interpreter. András had been a Fulbright recipient some years earlier, and had spent a year in America, teaching music in secondary schools in Pennsylvania. His English was impeccable, and he was/is a fabulous pianist! We became good friends, and he was the one primarily responsible for keeping me engaged with life in Pécs. He helped me with all the domestic needs of living there for a year, and took me to several sites . . . castles, museums, nature areas, etc. . . . in the region. Without András, my experience of my year in Hungary would have been quite different.

"People will try to tell you that all the great opportunities have been snapped up. In reality, the world changes every second, blowing new opportunities in all directions, including yours."
~ Ken Hakuta ~

For the conducting students, I worked with them as a class . . . first year students on one day; second year students on another. We used a couple of anthologies of piano music from Kodály and Bartók . . . with András as pianist . . . for musical material. These books contained a variety of short pieces, each with a different tempo, meter, style, and musical intent. As I remember, there were about ten students in each class (first year and second year). Their knowledge of analysis and form from their undergraduate diploma was quite good; much better than that of the average American student. So, we were able to work rather quickly, and made good progress through the year.

For the first year students, we focused primarily on the fundamentals of baton technique. The goal was to learn principles of technique which supported the concept of non-verbal communication. Simply put, we practiced physical gestures which would convey musical intent to an ensemble without the need for speaking. This is a common complaint in the conducting world . . . conductors talking and explaining what is needed in rehearsals, rather than physically reflecting the musical intent of the work at hand. Conductors do not speak during performances. It makes sense that they should develop the necessary non-verbal skills in rehearsals.

With the second year students, we worked mostly on score study skills during the fall semester … using a method taught to me by my mentor, David Whitwell. Maestro Whitwell learned this method from the legendary Austrian conductor and teacher, Hans Swarowsky, in Vienna. The conductor's score for a composition is somewhat akin to a blueprint for a building … it is not the actual music, only the symbol for the music. As such, one needs to develop the ability to translate that visual image (the score) to an aural image (the music). The printed notation for a piece of music can never accurately represent the complete musical idea that the composer imagined and felt. Thus, one must develop a means of discovering that which lies behind the printed score, to hear and feel what the composer heard and felt. Gustav Mahler once observed that "the best of music is not to be found in the notes."

The School of Music was also kind enough to schedule a chamber wind group … an octet … for me to work with for the year. My immediate supervisor was Károly Neumayer, a conductor and head of the wind faculty. I had been introduced to Károly during my first visit to Pécs several years before. I met with him during each of my subsequent visits, and we developed a close working relationship. He was able to smooth the way for all of the many new ideas and practices which I suggested through the year … he was always ready and willing to listen to an idea that would improve things for the students. Music ensembles, with a conductor, within the university curriculum was not a European tradition, though that has changed somewhat in recent years. I remember quite vividly my first introduction to the group, which we named Harmónia, the Hungarian spelling of Harmonie, a term given to the wind octets of the Classic period. Maestro Neumayer took me to the rehearsal room to meet the students. He informed me that we would meet twice weekly, for two hours each. When I asked about the dates of the concerts, the reply was, "Concerts?" They had scheduled rehearsals, but had not scheduled performances. We met with the head of the Music School about this, and he asked me, "Who would come to these concerts?" … to which I replied, "the public." They were bewildered; they could not imagine that the public would want to hear student performances! We were able to schedule several concerts through the year, and the faculty were quite surprised to find a large, and appreciative audience, for each performance. The repertoire was much the same as that performed with the Chamber Wind Players at UNI. When I returned to Pécs for a visit in 2007, I was thrilled to find that the ensemble had been retained in the curriculum!

One of my best, personal, memories of my time in Pécs was on Christmas Eve of that year. My friend, András, lives in the small village of Keszü, a few miles to the south of Pécs. The village church is quite beautiful, being built in 1781, and is the spiritual center of the village. There is not a resident priest for the church, but one that travels among several village churches in the region, and is available for Sunday masses and feast days. Each year, András arranges for a concert on Christmas Eve . . . the performers coming from the university in Pécs. The program, generally, is a mix of instrumentalists and singers, and is regarded as a special night among the people of the village. For that year, I was asked to be part of the festivities, and led the performers and the audience through a performance of the three-part round, "Dona Nobis Pacem." There was a short rehearsal involved with the audience, the text being printed in the programs. The three parts were separated among the audience members, and certain instruments assigned to each of the three parts. This came at the end of the night, and was a beautiful success. Everyone in the audience was also holding a candle in front of them, giving a warm glow to the ancient church, and the people. After the performance, a meal was served, along with wine and palinka. As we all left the church, there was a light, gentle, snow falling from the sky. The feeling among those present was one of great joy and gratitude . . . it was a quite lovely evening.

My Fulbright year in Hungary was one of the best years of my life. From my home in Pécs, I traveled to several other countries through the year . . . for professional, as well as cultural, occasions. These trips included visits to Normandy (France); Prague and Český Krumlov in the Czech Republic; Beijing and Shanghai in China; Croatia, and Italy. I also made numerous visits to cities and villages throughout Hungary. By the end of the year, I felt as comfortable

"The capacity for hope is the most significant fact of life. It provides human beings with a sense of destination and the energy to get started."
~ Norman Cousins ~

in Hungary as I did in Iowa ... maybe, even more so. I became
intimate with the Hungarian culture and traditions ... and grew
to love the country even more than before. From 1991 through 2005,
I was in Hungary at least once each year; she became my second
home. The people of Hungary ... their heritage, customs, and
traditions ... are among the finest in the world.

Of course, that year in Hungary had a major impact on my teaching
back in Iowa. I should mention that, as a consequence of my year
in Hungary, and my relationship with the Hungarian Fulbright
Commission, I was able to help two of our students (on separate
occasions) develop their own relationship with Mother Hungary.
In both cases, we were able to use my contacts as an entry point for
their studies ... one in percussion; the other in photography. From
that point, they made their own contacts, and formed ongoing
relationships with their Hungarian counterparts. Both students
have continued their relationships in Hungary, and continue to
return periodically for professional events.

The year of being apart from my work and the students at UNI gave
me an opportunity to reflect on our journey thus far; to consider
where we had been, and where we needed to go. In working with
the Hungarian students, and assisting their teachers in creating a
new paradigm, I was able to view the conditions and circumstances
at UNI with greater clarity. I could better see what was working
and what wasn't; where our strengths were, and where we needed
improvement. I slowly began to understand that I only had another
ten years or so before retirement. What was I going to do with
the time left? What needed to be done to secure conditions for
the legacy of the Wind Symphony to continue after I was gone?
What things were needed ... knowledge, information, activities,
experiences, and adventures ... for our students to have a more
complete education? These, and many more, were questions which
occupied my thinking during my time in Hungary. On my return
to Iowa, these questions remained. Answers and solutions came
in time, but never in complete form ... they were continually
changing; evolving ... transforming. But, from my view, the last
twelve years were the best.

Now that we were in our new home in the Gallagher-Bluedorn Performing Arts Center (GBPAC, or simply PAC), things began to move at an accelerated tempo with the Wind Symphony. Our continuing recruiting efforts were bringing many fine students to the School of Music. However, we were never able to completely solve all of our instrumental needs. Some years, we were flush with clarinets, both in quantity and quality, and deficient in double reeds. One year might bring several new trombonists, but no tubas. But, for the most part, the number of wind and percussion students needed for the Wind Symphony; the Symphony Orchestra, and the Symphonic Band . . . those began to stabilize, both in quantity and quality.

The Great Hall was a big lift for our annual band festival in February each year. In our new facility, we had more space for the many sessions scheduled for that event. And, we began a practice of inviting one of the outstanding bands in the state to come to campus and share a concert with the Wind Symphony. We made a day of it for them . . . rehearsal in the Great Hall; a campus tour, and dinner in the campus dining center across from the PAC. We had someone take photos of the band's visit, and gave them a recording of their evening performance. This was quite a hit with the teachers in the state, and we later expanded the idea to include the Symphonic Band in the venture. We asked our own university students to be part of the day, mostly helping with logistics. And, we asked them to do a short performance for the visiting high school students . . . both soloists and chamber groups. We thought that the most effective recruiting tactic was student to student. After they performed a short program, they talked with our visitors about what it was like to be a university student . . . information about dorm life, and study habits; musical and academic expectations, and other information that new students want to know, but usually don't ask. This was one of the most effective things we did in our many recruiting efforts.

After a few years of this, we initiated the Northern Iowa Band Invitational, a day long event, in March of each year, to which we invited five or six of the better band programs in the state to come and participate in a non-competitive event in the Great Hall. They were able to do a short warm-up in Davis Hall, and then have one hour on the Great Hall stage. The bands performed their program for part of that hour, and our conducting faculty worked with the bands in the time remaining. We also arranged campus tours for those schools which wanted it, and arranged for lunch in the dining center. The dining center was always a big event with the high school students, especially the variety of desserts! This was a quite successful event, and became an important part of our ongoing recruiting strategy.

IT WAS IN THIS FINAL PERIOD that the relationship between myself and the Wind Symphony began to find new and different dimensions . . . a deeper bond that allowed for more sincere and expressive music making. It didn't happen all at once, but gradually . . . sometimes small steps, sometimes larger ones.

It was during my Fulbright year (2004–05) in Hungary that I began to think more about how we might find deeper "human" connections in our music making; that the more we learned to support each other on a human level, the more powerful might become our mutual support on a musical level. It was about this time that I began the practice of appointing a *principal* player for each section. I had tried this earlier in my tenure, but we were not yet ready for the degree of involvement and commitment necessary for success. Now, I believed we were ready. The person appointed to this role was not always the "best" player in a particular section; maybe not even the oldest or one with more experience. But, in my judgment, she/he was the one with good personal skills, organizational skills, and the courage to lead.

"Be faithful to that which exists nowhere but in yourself."
~ André Gide ~

Of course, this developed over time. The younger players were able to observe what is needed for good section playing, and how the *principal* went about making that happen. Each year, the *principals* became more invested in their tasks, learning from the previous *principal*, and now adding their own thoughts and practices. Of course, I communicated regularly by email with them . . . asking for outside work on particular passages that we were preparing for performance. They would schedule regular section rehearsals, usually every week, in which they would work on essential ensemble skills ... intonation, blend, and balance. This, in addition to whatever work was needed for the technical demands of the performance repertoire.

The *principals* began to take the initiative to communicate with me about whatever problems (large or small) they might encounter. They began to arrange for gatherings of their section outside the needs of the ensemble ... a communal meal, watching a film together, etc. When I posted part assignments for the next concert, the section *principal* might meet with me if she/he felt that the distribution of parts was not equitable ... this player assigned to too many lower parts, and nothing on first. Or, that player is not quite ready for alto clarinet assignments ... let's wait until the spring.

In the final few years, I invited all of the *principals* for a meal (breakfast, lunch, or dinner) at the beginning of each semester ... and, usually again at the end. We met at a local restaurant, and talked about goals for the year, specific issues for the coming semester, and other items of importance. If it was a particularly busy year for us ... as in touring years ... we might meet more regularly. When we were preparing for a tour, the responsibilities for the *principals* increased substantially. Now, they needed to be "pack leader" ... making sure that all the players of their section were gathered at the right time, at the right place, with all the necessary items. They learned, through stories from the previous generation(s) of how to prepare for the tours ... how to take care of each other in case of illness, or other unforeseen circumstance.

By the end of my tenure, it would not have been possible to do all the things that we were able to accomplish together ... nor, as well as we were able to do what we did ... without the support and commitment of the *principal players*. After all these many years ... thinking about what might have been if we started this tradition earlier ... I am still not sure if we had to wait for *them* to develop, or for *me* to develop. Maybe, it doesn't matter ... maybe, it all happened exactly as it was supposed to happen.

ANOTHER TRADITION that we started right around the time of my return from Hungary, was the custom of using the last rehearsal of the semester as an occasion to say goodbye to those who were leaving us . . . either by graduation, or for student teaching/internship in the following semester. We also started to compile a "memory book" at the end of each academic year. In the final few weeks, I would ask the players to send me, by email, their thoughts and feelings on the year just ending . . . reflections on personal growth, ensemble growth, unforgettable moments, whatever they wished to contribute. I would collect all of the thoughts and memories, and create a "book" which also included the season's repertoire, performance dates, guest soloists, and whatever comments I might have received from audience members, the faculty, or alumni. We would have this printed and bound by the university print services folks, and distribute at the final rehearsal period.

I would begin with comments about the year or semester just finished, and offer a few thoughts on the coming semester or year. Most often, I included some poetry interspersed through my comments . . . reading poems which spoke to the human condition, or whose message might offer hope and inspiration. Then, we would speak to those who were leaving us. There were usually ten to twelve members leaving each semester. One by one, I would offer my thoughts on their time with us . . . perhaps relating some personal remembrance, or noting the person's growth and development . . . expressing my appreciation for her/his contributions to the ensemble, and offering best wishes for their future. Then, I would ask them to speak . . . asking about their immediate future: where would they do their internship; did they have a position waiting for them, etc. Next, their colleagues spoke to them . . . telling of personal stories they shared; maybe speaking of their human qualities that were admired. And, finally, the student spoke to us . . . reflecting on what the many friendships and their relationship with the Wind Symphony had meant to them. It generally was an emotional time, often tearful for some. I was always touched by the care and sincerity with which everyone spoke. This was a moment . . . if only a small, and maybe fleeting one . . . in which we all recognized that something was changing; we would be different after today; a few of us would be absent at the next gathering. These times are among the most treasured of my memories with these wonderful people . . . and, I believe, for each of them, also.

WE ALSO INSTITUTED the tradition of selecting the *Outstanding Musician* from the Wind Symphony at the close of each academic year. Again, from my time of reflection in Hungary, I came to believe that we needed some visible means of acknowledging the pursuit of excellence exhibited by our students . . . a way to honor their efforts in the areas of musicianship, scholarship, and leadership. So, we created the Wind Symphony Outstanding Musician Award . . . an annual award presented to the player who represented the highest standards of the practices and traditions of the Wind Symphony.

Figure 15: UNI Wind Symphony Outstanding Musician Award criteria

**Wind Symphony
Outstanding Musician**

2016–2017

This person should represent
The highest standards of:

Performing, Creative, and Scholarly Excellence

Service and Support for Colleagues

Leadership

This person should embody
the traditions, intentions, and ambitions
which you want associated with the
Northern Iowa Wind Symphony

This was a player selected, entirely, by vote of the students. Initially, we included the other members of the conducting faculty as consultants in the process . . . allowing for the possibility that the student vote might reflect more of a "popularity contest," rather than the person who best represents those qualities indicated above. It was a needless worry . . . the players chose correctly every time. In some years, there were two, or even three, outstanding players receiving the same, or almost the same, number of votes. Rather than arbitrarily selecting a single player, perhaps based on my own preferences, I decided to make the award according to the preferences of the ensemble.

I waited until the evening of our final concert to announce the recipient(s) of each year's award. I usually did this right at the beginning of the second half. They were presented with a plaque which indicated the person's name, the title of the award, and the academic year of the award. We also installed a larger plaque in a glass case in Davis Hall, our rehearsal space. On this plaque were the names of each recipient, and the year of the award. While the practice of recognizing outstanding musicians each year came to an end in the spring of 2017, following my retirement, the plaque recognizing those so honored has remained in Davis Hall.

My only regret with this practice is that I didn't start this tradition when I first arrived thirty-five years ago.

Figure 16: UNI Wind Symphony Outstanding Musician Award, 2009–2017, recipients

2009–2010	Andrew Hamilton, horn
2010–2011	Aaron Hynds, tuba
2011–2012	Kristin Conrad, percussion
	Betsy Groat, flute
	James Gummert, clarinet
2012–2013	Nicolas Addelia, percussion
	Elizabeth Kreassig, flute
2013–2014	Erin Maltby, trumpet
	Jillian Whitaker, saxophone
	Nicholas Wills, horn
2014–2015	Hayley Graham, clarinet
	Michael Prichard, trumpet
2015–2016	Brent Mead, trombone
2016–2017	Michelle Meadows, flute

Table 5: Recipients of the UNI Wind Symphony Outstanding Musician Award, 2009–2017

ONE OF THE MORE SIGNIFICANT DEVELOPMENTS in this final part of our history was the creation of the Iowa Band Conductors Forum. In the summer of 2012, I invited the conductors at Drake University (Robert Meunier), Iowa State University (Michael Golemo), and the University of Iowa (Mark Heidel) to meet with the intention of creating a new paradigm for assisting young conductors, at whatever level, in their efforts to develop the knowledge and skills necessary for effective and expressive music-making. We met at the home of Maestro Meunier in Des Moines, and discussed possibilities for several hours. Earlier, I had sent them a message outlining my thoughts and hopes for a new forum in which we might create a program in which the four of us together could be more effective than we could as individuals. I was the only one of the four that had been part of the National Wind Ensemble Conferences in the 1970s, and used that as a model for what I hoped we could create. I proposed a 1 1/2–2 day weekend event which focused solely on the art and craft of music making . . . no organization, no officers, no dues, no members, no committees . . . only music making. The idea was immediately welcomed by the other three, and we set about creating the Iowa Band Conductors Forum.

We continued to talk and plan through the 2012–13 academic year, and announced our plans to the membership of the Iowa

Bandmasters Association at their annual conference in May of 2013. In a special session, just for this occasion, the four of us sat together for a panel to explain the ideas behind the Forum, and answered questions regarding its impetus. This marked the first time that the conductors of the four major universities in the state had appeared together in a public forum. One of the benefits of our partnership was something we had not planned for . . . it reduced the "tribal" tendencies of our graduates. Now, an alumnus of one school need not be burdened with feeling that they should disregard, or give little attention to, the comments and teaching philosophies of the conductors at the other three schools. Over the years, on the occasions of the Forum, the band conductors in attendance came to see the genuine respect and admiration among the four of us . . . we liked each other, and were friends!

JANUARY 24 & 25, 2014
Iowa Band Conductors Forum

Richard Mark Heidel
University of Iowa

Michael Golemo
Iowa State University

Ronald Johnson
University of Northern Iowa

Robert Meunier
Drake University

FRIDAY JANUARY 24

2:00-3:30	Mark Heidel, *"Back to Basics"*
3:30	break
3:45-5:15	Ronald Johnson, *"Rediscovering Gustav (von) Holst"*
5:30-:6:30	complimentary dinner for all participants
6:45-8:00	Randy Hogancamp, *"Taiko Drumming"* (all participants)
8:00	break
8:15-9:45	Panel Discussion: *"Repertoire as Curriculum"*

SATURDAY JANUARY 25

9:00- 12:00	Conducting Seminar (12 invited conductors, see info below)
12:15-1:15	complimentary lunch for all participants
1:30-3:00	Robert Meunier, *"Who, What, Why, Where, When and How: A Student-Centered Approach to the Rehearsal Hall"*
3:00	break
3:15-4:45	Michael Golemo *"Making Marches Musical"*
4:45	Wrap-up

School of Music
University of Northern Iowa

Iowa Band Conductors Forum

*A shared initiative among the four universities . . .
envisioned as a forum for presentations, discussions
and activities focused on the Art of Conducting*

Session topics will include rehearsal tactics and strategies, rehearsal planning, repertoire, performance practices and a conducting seminar. Ensembles for *Forum* sessions will be the **Northern Iowa Wind Symphony** and **Symphonic Band.**

The *Forum* is available to conductors and teachers at all levels: middle school, high school and college/university.

The *Forum* is offered at no cost to participants. However, we do ask that you let us know (by response to this message) that you are coming. We need to plan for the Friday evening meal and Saturday lunch (complimentary for all participants).

Saturday Conducting Seminar

The seminar is available for 12 conductors. The rehearsal ensemble will be the *Northern Iowa Wind Symphony.* If you are interested in this opportunity, please be in contact with one of the *Forum* hosts:

Michael Golemo, Mark Heidel, Ronald Johnson or Robert Meunier.

There has been substantial interest in the *Forum* expressed since our announcement at the IBA Convention in May. While there is no limit to the number of participants we can accommodate, we do recommend that you let us know of your intentions as soon as possible.

**School of Music
University of Northern Iowa**

We agreed that the Forum would rotate among the four universities, but that the four of us would collectively determine the format and content of each year's event. We chose the next-to-last weekend in January as the best time for the event . . . that seemed the best time so as not to interfere with most other events in the state scheduled for the spring. We decided that each of the four conductors would offer a presentation on a topic of their choice . . . with or without a live ensemble. The topics could include rehearsal strategies, repertoire, philosophical inquiry . . . whatever we felt was helpful to the mission of improving the art of music-making. There would be a conducting session with the university's premier ensemble, with twelve high school conductors each getting fifteen minutes of podium time. These twelve were coached by one of the four of us, in rotation, with the other three writing comments and suggestions, or making verbal comments on the video tape that would be given to each conductor. We also agreed to provide the evening meal on Friday, and lunch on Saturday for all of the participants.

As of this writing, the Iowa Band Conductors Forum continues to be an enormous success for the band conductors in the state. The first offering was in January of 2014, held on the campus of the University of Northern Iowa. The following year was at Iowa State University, with Drake University hosting in 2016, and the University of Iowa in 2017. The event returned to Northern Iowa in 2018, starting a new round of offerings. There were about forty teacher/conductors who attended in 2014, about sixty in 2015, and similar numbers in 2016 and 2017. The written comments gathered at the conclusion of each year's event indicated that this was a much needed event, one which focused only on the art of expressive music-making, rather than other, often non-musical, issues which are offered in other conferences and conventions.

It was our (the original four of us) collective hope . . . certainly mine . . . that the Forum would become an event that actually made a difference for those who attended; that it would not only instruct, but also inspire. And, we hoped that it would continue to exist long after any one of us was retired from the profession. So far, that has been true.

THE 2016–2017 ACADEMIC YEAR was my final one with the Wind Symphony. At that time, the University had an unusual policy of hiring only one-year, temporary, replacements for faculty who retired, or left for a position elsewhere. The year following the resignation was then used for a national search to find a new person for the vacated position. So, I formally resigned at the close of the spring semester of 2016, but remained for the following academic year, only conducting the Wind Symphony ... becoming, in effect, my own temporary replacement. This, in an attempt to promote a less disruptive transition from my departure to the arrival of my successor.

For this final season, I wanted to program works which represented the history and traditions of the previous thirty-four years with the Wind Symphony. Thus, I chose pieces from composers that were close to me, and close to the Wind Symphony ... Karel Husa, Leonard Bernstein, and Percy Grainger. There were pieces which were new to the ensemble, but in keeping with our history and traditions ... David Maslanka, Timo Forsström (Finland), and Satoshi Yagisawa (Japan). And, we were able to commission several new pieces for this final season. David Whitwell composed the second movement, "Faith," of his *Symphony No. 6* for us. Two former students composed pieces for the occasion ... Isaac Brockshus (*reset*) and Jillian Whitaker (*Coming Home*). Daniel Bukvich had told me the in previous year that he wanted to compose a work for the occasion of my retirement. He gave us *Symphonic Movement*, a spectacular composition which I mentioned earlier in this text. And, Rolf Rudin (Germany), composed a most special piece for the Wind Symphony and the Varsity Men's Glee Club, entitled *Te Deum*, op. 93. It is a brilliant piece of music and, as of this writing, the only setting of the Te Deum text for male chorus and wind orchestra. Funding for Mr. Rudin's commission came from the School of Music and the Varsity Men's Glee Club.

With encouragement, and funding from the School of Music, we hosted the Midwest International Conducting Symposium in March of 2017. We invited five talented young conductors from northern Italy to come for a week of study with myself, Dr. Burkhardt, and Danny Galyen, conductor of the Symphonic Band at that time. Claudio Re also came to assist with the program, and help with translations when needed. The invited conductors were Stefano Giacomelli, Marta Lecchi, Davide Sottini, Erina Ferrarini, and Marco Rampini. Each of the conductors had rehearsal time with the Wind Symphony and Symphony Orchestra on Monday and Wednesday, and with the Symphonic Band on Tuesday. We scheduled the Northern Iowa Band Invitational for Thursday of that week (all day), and our guests were involved with that. We also had several sessions with score study strategies, repertoire sessions, and short wind music history sessions. They were also involved with the West African Drumming Ensemble (WADE), and some Taiko drumming. In the evenings, there were recitals to attend and social occasions with our university students. It was a memorable week for everyone!

The final concert for the Wind Symphony was scheduled for April 21, 2017, at Urbandale High School, near Des Moines. In our initial planning and scheduling in the previous year, it was not possible, during the month of April, to find a weekend date in the Great Hall for our performance. So, we had to look for an off-campus site. At some point after the initial scheduling, it was determined that it would be possible to schedule a second performance in the Great Hall on Monday, the 24th of April.

We also wanted to close my tenure at Northern Iowa with a reunion of alumni players who had performed with the Wind Symphony during their student days. Thus, we scheduled the 35th Anniversary Reunion of the Wind Symphony for that weekend. The university Alumni Association scheduled an event for the concert in Urbandale on Friday, as we have many alumni teaching and working in the Des Moines area.

On Saturday afternoon, we had a recital of performances by former students, who returned for this occasion. There were students who now held university teaching positions around the country; players pursuing professional careers with symphony orchestras, ballet orchestras, and military bands. And, we had many students who enjoyed successful careers in public school teaching. In the evening, we had a catered meal in the foyer of the Gallagher-Bluedorn Performing Arts Center. At the end, I gave my farewell address to the group, thanking them for helping to create the "Wind Symphony family," and for their significant contributions to my career, and to my personal life. We then retired to one of several local establishments, where we continued the reunion.

On Sunday afternoon, we had a rehearsal for all those who had returned, playing through several of our favorites from times gone by. The next night, the Wind Symphony performed its final concert for a large and enthusiastic audience. One can find that performance on YouTube ... Jillian Whitaker: *Coming Home*, Daniel Bukvich: *Symphonic Movement*, Timo Forsström: *Sons of the Midnight Sun*, and Rolf Rudin: *Te Deum*, op. 93.

Concert Tours

WHEN I FIRST ARRIVED IN 1982, previous custom had been that the Wind Ensemble took a short tour each year, to perform in high schools around the state. Jazz Band One also toured, but no other ensembles ... not the orchestra or the chorus. As I understood the custom, the group traveled in the week prior to the band festival in February, with the Friday festival concert being the final one. It was/is my belief that we should not take students out of classes without a good reason; that we should do so only when other options are exhausted. And, that the reason for taking students away from scheduled classes should be of sufficient value to warrant their absence. So, we began to take those tours during the university's spring break in mid-March. As with most other university touring ensembles of that period, we scheduled performances in high schools around the state; usually two performances each day ... the one in the evening often being shared with the local school's band. The students were given meals at the schools, and often were lodged with host families at night. The tour usually only lasted for three or four days, so that students could still have some portion of the spring break to rest and catch up on sleep.

At that time, tours were believed to be an important factor in the recruitment of new students into the university. So, the task was to identify the strong high school music programs in the state, and schedule performances there. We also took trips to schools in Missouri, Illinois, and Minnesota. Each year, it became more and more difficult to schedule performances at high schools ...

the idea of families hosting students overnight was fading and hotels for the students were expensive. As always ... "times were a changin'," and after a few years of this practice, I started to look for a different, more effective recruitment strategy. I was also a bit embarrassed that the Wind Symphony was the only concert ensemble that was allotted funds for touring. So, right around 1989 or so, we created a rotation system that allowed the Orchestra and the Concert Chorale to also take tours. This meant that the Wind Symphony only went out every third year. A few years after this, owing to funding changes (funding is always a problem!), Jazz Band One joined in the rotation ... allowing each ensemble to tour every four years. That system has remained in effect to the present.

By the start of the 1990s, the Wind Symphony had mostly stopped in-state tours in which we performed at high schools for three or four days. Occasionally, we would do a "run-out," leaving campus around 4:00 PM and driving to a town within an hour's drive, play an evening concert ... either us alone, or shared with the school band ... and return to campus that evening. As a recruitment factor, we found more success in inviting one of the better high school bands in the state to come to our campus, and share a concert with the Wind Symphony. It is well known that high school students are more attracted to a university where they have visited the campus, and had a good experience there. We did that for several years, and found that the high school conductors, and their students, responded quite favorably, especially after the Performing Arts Center was completed (2000), and the Great Hall became our concert home.

IN THE SUMMER OF 1989, my friend and mentor, David Whitwell, invited me to serve as guest conductor for his final European concert tour with the California State University, Northridge, Wind Ensemble. He also invited twelve or so of our players to be part of that ensemble, as several of the CSUN players were not able to make the trip. It was my first trip to Europe; also for our students. I rehearsed the repertoire with our students as much as possible, making sure we were ready to put the group together

at our first stop in Switzerland. It was a two-week tour, with
performances in Switzerland, Italy, Germany, Luxembourg, and
the Netherlands. The final performance was on the occasion of the
biennial conference of the World Association of Symphonic Bands
and Ensembles (WASBE) in Kerkrade in the Netherlands. This
conference was linked to the annual occasion of the World Music
Contest (WMC), perhaps the most famous event for wind music
in Europe. The tour was a marvelous experience, and whetted my
appetite for more. I made several friends during this excursion,
and when I returned to Iowa, I began corresponding by mail with
each of them, further developing the relationships. When I had my
first sabbatical in 1991, I was able to visit with several of these new
friends, and began to think seriously about the possibility of our
own students ... the Wind Symphony ... making a concert tour in
Europe.

Hungary, 1993

OUR FIRST EUROPEAN TOUR WAS TO HUNGARY, in March of 1993. The invitation came as a result of my visits to Hungary during my first sabbatical in the spring of 1991, and again during my return visit in the spring of 1992. I had been invited to conduct rehearsals and concerts with the wind orchestra of the Hungarian Customs and Finance Administration in March of that year. On this occasion, my visit was somewhat like a "state visit," as it coincided with two major events ... the annual March 15 celebration of the Hungarian Revolution of 1848, and the 125th anniversary of the founding of the Hungarian Customs and Finance Administration. In this context, I was invited to attend many of the official events of both celebrations. I was even introduced to the President of Hungary, Árpád Göncz. It was a most memorable week!

During one of several meals with the Cultural Affairs folks of the Customs and Finance Administration, we discussed the possibility of bringing the Wind Symphony to Hungary for a concert tour. I was very excited by this opportunity, and there were several more discussions on the subject. Through an "unofficial" interpreter, it was determined that the Wind Symphony would be invited as guests of the Customs Administration for a week in March of 1993, during our spring break. It was further suggested that, at some time in the future, should the wind orchestra of the Customs Administration be able to come to America, that I would help to arrange concerts and logistics for their trip. Of course, I quickly agreed!

I returned to Iowa, and immediately began to make preparations for the trip. This was, again, a time before email and the internet— all correspondence was in written form with traditional international postal service. As I began to request assistance for ground transportation, lodging, and meals, I was told that all of this would be handled by the Customs Administration ... we would be their official guests! I was stunned ... this was really quite a major event! Our only expense would be airfare from Iowa to Budapest.

However, over the next several months, I began to get nervous about the progress with details, especially the number of concerts we would perform. I wanted five or six, and our hosts were only suggesting one or two. So, during the Thanksgiving break in November, I flew to Budapest to see if I could make better progress in person. It was during one of several marvelous dinners that I ... we ... discovered that a critical mistake had been made in translation during the original discussions in the previous spring. What the Customs Administration was offering was an "official exchange program" ... they would take care of arrangements and expenses for our visit to Hungary, and, in return, we (the University of Northern Iowa) would do the same for their trip to America. Obviously, that was not possible for us, and the realization of this mistake cast a pall over the evening. I was to be their guest at the opera that night, Puccini's *La Bohemé*, and they suggested that I go to the opera, and we would discuss the situation the next day. The person in charge, part of the Cultural Affairs department, said very gently (paraphrased), "Don't worry, Ronald. We prefer consultation rather than confrontation. We will find a solution." It was a wonderful thing to say, and a trait of the Hungarian people that I found on all of my subsequent visits. From that moment, I have tried to adopt that attitude into all of my professional negotiations.

The final resolution of the situation was that the Customs Administration made all the arrangements for ground transportation (bus), lodging, and meals, but all of those costs were paid by us. That seemed a reasonable and appropriate accommodation ... an arrangement for which I had originally expected and planned. With financial support from the School of Music, and other sources within the University, the students only paid about $800 for the trip.

THE TRIP WAS FROM MARCH 15 until the 21st, in 1993. We performed four concerts ... in a lovely concert hall in the city of Egér, at the Franz Liszt Academy of Music, another concert shared with two Hungarian bands in a Budapest suburb, and a live broadcast over Hungarian National Radio (the Bartók Channel!).

We took an international repertoire:

Karel Husa (Czech Republic/USA)	*Smetana Fanfare*
Frigyes Hidas (Hungary)	*Concertino Fúvószenekarra*
Noel Stockton (South Africa)	*Manguang*
Daniel Bukvich (USA)	*The Dream of Abraham* (ms)
Árpád Balázs (Hungary)	*Fanfárverbunk*
Bernard van Beurden (Netherlands)	*Concerto for Bassoon, Winds and Percussion*
Guy Woolfenden (England)	*Gallimaufry*
Joaquin Rodrigo (Spain)	*Adagio para Orquestra de Instrumentos de Viento*
Percy Aldridge Grainger (Australia/USA)	*Country Gardens*
	Colonial Song
	The Gumsuckers

Table 6: Hungary 1993 tour repertoire

Our week in Hungary began with a Conducting Seminar for Hungarian conductors, using the Wind Symphony as the rehearsal ensemble. The rehearsal facility for the wind orchestra of the Customs Administration was used for the occasion. There were about a dozen, or so, young conductors from various parts of the country. We developed many good friends during the seminar, and our reputation began to spread as a result of both the seminar and our performances. Our newly established prestige was to be quite helpful when planning for the tours in 1996, and 2000.

We also enjoyed a visit to a *puszta* ... a sort of Hungarian "ranch" on the eastern plains of Hungary, the Hortobágy. The place was the home of an internationally known artist, Ferenc Polyac, whose specialty was carving wooden sculptures ... of people, animals, and even landscapes. He created a wonderful meal for us, with the Hungarian national dish, *gulyás* (goulash), being the main course.

Our hosts also arranged for us to be part of the annual March 15 national holiday, celebrating the 1848 Revolution against the Austrian Empire. It was a solemn and emotional event which touched each of us. Later, a special tour of the Parliament building was arranged for us, and we were guests for a performance of Richard Wagner's opera, *Das Rheingold*, at the Budapest Opera House.

Figure 17: Hungary 1993 tour poster

David Rachor, our Professor of Bassoon, came along with us as soloist. The Dutch composer, Bernard van Beurden, had composed a concerto for solo bassoon and large chamber ensemble especially for this occasion in Hungary, the *Concerto for Bassoon, Winds and Percussion*. Thomas Tritle, the Professor of Horn at that time, also was with us to perform Franz Krommer's *Concerto in E-flat for Two Horns*. Our principal hornist, Valerie Lueders, joined him for this occasion. These concerti were the two featured works in our radio broadcast over the Bartók Channel of the Hungarian National Radio (Magyar Rádió). Our hosts told us that our performance was heard by an estimated three million listeners … a once-in-a-lifetime experience for both the group and the University of Northern Iowa!

Figure 18: Hungarian National Radio, Studio 1

Our concert in the Liszt Academy represented the first-ever performance by an American university wind orchestra in that historic concert hall. This is a space where Brahms had performed … and Toscanini, and Bernstein, and so many other wonderful musicians from our history. The acoustics were impeccable, and the audience was near capacity for our concert. We were told that this was also the first occasion for wind music of Percy Grainger to be performed in Hungary. I was quite pleased by this news, and was thrilled by the exuberant reception of our performance.

The center piece for the program was Daniel Bukvich's *The Dream of Abraham*. This was a piece that Dan had composed especially for the Wind Symphony, and our visit to Hungary. The inspiration for the work came from Dan's remembrance of, and reflection on, the events and circumstances surrounding the assassination of President John Fitzgerald Kennedy on 22 November, 1963. It was also much influenced by the 8mm film recording of the assassination by Abraham Zapruder. The piece uses vocal sounds from the players, and other musical symbolism ... 22-beat rhythmic patterns; 6/3 chord inversions ... temple blocks representing the sound of horse's hooves during the funeral cortege, and funeral calls from a solo trumpet. It is a remarkable work; quite powerful and emotionally exhausting.[19]

The piece was the final work performed before the intermission. President Kennedy was much admired by the Hungarian people ... indeed, most of the world. The passage of time had not diminished their admiration and respect for this great American. When we finished the piece, there was no applause ... only silence! After a few moments, I left the stage, and motioned for the players to follow. When we returned for the second half, we were met with thunderous applause ... a standing ovation! The Hungarians had considered the piece as a memorial for President Kennedy ... more like a "eulogy," and felt that applause immediately after the performance would have been inappropriate. It was an emotional moment for us, and one that I will never forget. In subsequent visits, I often met people who had heard that performance, and they always referred to this piece ... "the Memory for Mr. Kennedy."

[19] One can find more information about the piece, and a recording (our performance!) on Dan's website: www.bukvichmusic.com

Figure 19: Northern Iowa Wind Symphony performing in the Franz Liszt Academy of Music

Hungary, 1996

OUR SECOND TRIP TO HUNGARY was in the spring of 1996, March 10–16. By this time, I was much more aware of the traditions and customs of Hungary, and had formed relationships with many more friends. On several occasions, I was a guest of the Hungarian Army, and their Music School in Budapest . . . being invited to work with their percussionists. This was a truly delightful experience . . . my several visits included gatherings and conferences with several universities in the country where there were strong percussion programs. And, I had met several of the conductors of the better wind orchestras in the country. So, we were accorded celebrity status in each of our performance venues. The tour was sponsored by the Hungarian Wind Music Association—an organization of composers, conductors, and other music professionals.

Figure 20: Wind Symphony players at Fisherman's Bastion in the Castle District of Budapest.

The repertoire for this trip was:

Table 7: Hungary 1996 tour repertoire

Nikolai Rimsky-Korsakov (Russia)	*Cortege aus "Mlada"*
Ron Nelson (USA)	*Medieval Suite*
Daniel Bukvich (USA)	*Meditations on the Writings of Vasily Kandinsky*
György Rankí (Hungary)	*Suite from Pomádé Király Uj Ruhája*
Gustav Mahler (Austria)	*Um Mitternacht*
David Whitwell (USA)	*Sinfonia da Requiem, in memory of Mozart*

The Director of the School of Music, Raymond Tymas-Jones, came along as soloist for Gustav Mahler's beautiful lied, *Um Mitternacht* (At Midnight). And, Jeffrey Funderburk, our Professor of Tuba and Euphonium, was soloist with Dan Bukvich's *Meditations on the Writings of Vasily Kandinsky*. This is a work commissioned by Dr. Funderburk, especially for this concert tour. Each of Dan's compositions is unique . . . each work being unlike any of his previous pieces. This one is no exception. The printed notation is the same for everyone . . . conductor, soloist, and players. The "harmony" is created by the different keys in which each instrument is tuned . . . horns in F, trumpets in B-flat (also E-flat, D, and A), clarinets in B-flat, alto saxophone in E-flat, flute and piccolo in C . . . etc., etc.[20]

There were five performances . . . Abony, Békéscsaba, Budapest (Franz Liszt Academy of Music), Csolnok, and Makó. In the time since our tour in 1993, and with my own personal travels there each year, the Wind Symphony had become quite well-known in Hungary. Each of the concerts was unique . . . each performance was met by capacity crowds, warm hospitality, and great memories. But, the two most memorable evenings were those in Csolnok and Makó.

Csolnok is a small village about sixty miles northwest of Budapest. At the time of our visit, it was a village of about 2,500 residents, with a history of coal mining. The village dates from the thirteenth century, but was completely destroyed in 1696 during the Turkish occupation. After its destruction, the King of Hungary, Leopold I, invited German families from the Alsace, Rhineland, and Bavaria regions to resettle in the area around Csolnok. The German influence remains to this day. All public notices are printed in both Hungarian and German . . . the German name for the village being Tscholnok.

We arrived in the village in the early afternoon, and were met by the town council and other village leaders. We were taken on a short tour of the village, and were invited to visit many of the family wine cellars in the village. Hungary has a long tradition of wine making, almost every family makes its own wine. Though the students were not permitted to sample the wines before performances, the courteous and hospitable villagers made sure that everyone had a bottle of their wine to take with them as a memory of their time in Csolnok. We had a short rehearsal at the performance site . . . a community center/sports hall . . . and a small snack arranged by the town council before the performance. There was a banquet planned for after the concert . . . the entree being the famous Hungarian *gulyás* (goulash). The best hunter of the village had gone into the forest that morning to harvest a deer for the *gulyás*.

[20] The audio recording of our performance in Budapest is available on YouTube (https://youtu.be/etMs-tu3d84), along with the printed notation.

Figure 21: 1996 Hungary tour poster

The performance in the evening was excellent, it seemed that the entire village was present . . . each piece was greeted with warm and enthusiastic applause. The final work on the program was Maestro Whitwell's *Sinfonia da Requiem, in memory of Mozart.* The work is one of my personal favorites, and one which was very dear to the students. They always poured their emotions into the music . . . it was always a special moment for both the players and the audience.

When the concert was over, many people from the audience came to thank the players, and perhaps get an autograph on their program. The people were so kind and enthusiastic, it was a warm atmosphere. The students took care of loading their instruments . . . along with the percussion equipment we brought along . . . on to the bus, and headed to the place where the banquet would be held. I was kept busy with greeting people, and signing autographs. Again, the people were so very courteous and appreciative.

Figure 22: The Wind Symphony at Acquincum, the old Roman capital of Pannonia province.

Finally, the hall was empty, and I headed to the banquet. As I stepped outside the door leading to the other building, I noticed a small group of people standing over an elderly woman, sitting in a chair. The woman looked as though she had fainted. I asked, "Is she okay?" One of the young men said, in English, "No, she has died." When I looked closer, I could see that was true. I said something like, "I am so very sorry, is there something I can do?" "No," the young man replied, "we are waiting for the police." The village was so remote that there was no medical facility in the village, and no police assigned to the town. Again, I said, "I am very sorry for your loss." The young man said, "It is okay. All of her family was with her tonight. She had a good life, and she was listening to beautiful music when she died. Thank you for what you gave to her." My eyes were filled with tears now. I shook the young man's hand, and turned away to walk to the banquet, only a couple of minutes away.

When I arrived, I was met by the leader of the town council . . . the students had already been informed of what had happened. He told me what I had just learned, and said that our hosts were needed to take care of the woman who had died, and give comfort to the family. The tables were set for a splendid meal, with all kinds of traditional dishes and pastries, and, of course, bottles of the village wine. I could see that the students were quite distressed by what had happened. So, I told them of my conversation with the young man outside the concert hall. We talked a bit about the power of music, and the gift that we are able to give to those who were present that night. We quietly enjoyed the meal that had been prepared for us and, when finished, boarded the bus for the trip back to Budapest. It was a moment that none of us will ever forget.

The other special night for us was in Makó, in the southeast part of Hungary. It is near to Szeged, where there is a university with a very fine music department. Many of the music students from the university performed with the Makó community band, which was quite excellent! We arrived around lunch time, and were greeted by the Mayor and town council . . . along with young children in traditional Hungarian attire, singing and dancing traditional Hungarian folk songs. It was a most joyous occasion! We were given an excellent meal, and taken on a short tour of the town.

The concert that evening was shared with the community band of Makó . . . again, a very fine ensemble. The performance site was not especially large, but they had arranged for a large screen for remote viewing in another building close by. All together there were perhaps 700–800 people in attendance that evening. And, again, it was a most enthusiastic reception from the audience. The performance was filmed by the regional television facility for later broadcast. It was quite an excellent production, using four or five cameras. I am told that it was broadcast (Magyar Televízió) on several occasions after our departure. Each time that I returned to Hungary, I quite often met someone who was present for that concert, or heard it on television.

The Hungarian people have a unique way of applauding in concerts. When the piece is finished and is well received, the audience begins to applaud ... but, very quickly, some group of people begin with slow, single, claps, immediately joined by the rest of the audience: clap . . . . . . clap . . . . . clap . . . . clap . . . clap . . clap, accelerating until there is frenzied, enthusiastic, applause. After a short while, somewhere in the audience, the cycle would start again. It might be repeated several times, depending on their enthusiasm for the performance. For this performance, we played every piece of music we had in the folders, and still they asked for more. Finally, after repeated bows and acknowledgements, I took the hand of one of the flute players, and motioned for the rest to follow off stage. It was a magnificent evening!

This tour had a much different character to it than did the journey in 1993. I had more experience with the culture and the language, and our hosts were more familiar with the ensemble ... by way of the "musicians' grapevine" which seems to exist in every country, and my several professional visits since our last visit. Our final performance was in the famed Liszt Academy of Music. Our performance was recorded by the engineers of Hungarian National Radio, and became the basis for our compact disc recording, *Requiem*. We had a day for sightseeing and shopping in the castle district, high on the cliffs of the Buda side, overlooking the Danube. And, on the final night, we had a lovely "Hungarian Style" banquet in the hotel where we were staying ... complete with traditional Hungarian folk music and dancing. And, it was a great honor to have our wonderful friends ... Maestro Lendvay, Frici Bacsi (Mr. Hidas), and László Marosi ... as our special guests for the evening. It was an unforgettable end to an unforgettable adventure!

Hungary, 2000

OUR FINAL ADVENTURE IN HUNGARY was in the spring of 2000, again during the university's spring break . . . March 9–18. We performed concerts in Bóly, Budapest, Kiskunfélegyháza, Makó, and Pécs. My good friend, Imre Bogyó, made all the arrangements for this last tour. Imre is a musician (pianist) and arts promoter with whom I had met earlier, and worked with him on several projects. He put together an exceptional tour for us . . . again, with wonderful audiences and great adventures.

I chose an "American" program for this trip:

Clifton Williams	*Symphonic Dance No. 3, "Fiesta"*
Aaron Copland	*Suite from "The Red Pony"*
Robert Russell Bennett	*Rose Variations*
Edward MacDowell	*Woodland Sketches*
Bruce Broughton	*Excursions for Trumpet and Band*
Daniel Bukvich	*Unusual Behavior in Ceremonies Involving Drums*

Table 8: Hungary 2000 tour repertoire

Randy Grabowski, our Professor of Trumpet, came with us as soloist. And, he offered masterclasses for Hungarian trumpet players in Budapest and Makó. As with the previous two tours, this adventure was truly remarkable! I was much more familiar with the customs and traditions of the Hungarian people, and the reputation of the Wind Symphony was quite well known in the country.

Our first performance was in the city of Kiskunfélegyháza, about one hundred miles south of Budapest, and close to the city of Kecskemét, home for the Kodály Institute, and birthplace for the famous composer and music educator, Zoltán Kodály. Kiskunfélegy-háza has long enjoyed a tradition of having a very fine community band, with whom we shared the concert. We were there for two days, hosted by families in the community . . . a real treat for the students. On the first day, we were taken to a *puszta* near the village of Bugac, where we were treated to an excellent meal of Hungarian *gulyás*, tasty desserts, and the excellent local wine. After the meal, we enjoyed a horse show of the local Csikós ... the famous mounted horse-herdsmen of Hungary. And, our hosts arranged for me to sit on one of the horses ... an occasion from which all of the students had a photo! What great memories!

Figure 23: The Wind Symphony with Hungarian Csikós

Figure 24: Hungarian Csikós

The next day, we had a short tour of the town, and a rehearsal in the concert facility. The concert that evening was excellent. The hall was filled with an enthusiastic audience, who asked for several encores. Our visit in Kiskunfélegyháza was a grand beginning for our tour.

Our visit to the small village of Bóly was quite memorable. Bóly is situated in one of the major wine producing regions of Hungary. And, it is quite near to Mohács, the site of two historic battles against the Ottoman Empire ... the first in 1526, and the second in 1687. These were pivotal battles in the long history of Hungary, and the resulting loss of many thousands of its people severely affected its development. In the hearts and minds of Hungarians, Mohács is similar to what Gettysburg means to Americans.

Apparently, when our friend, Imre, initially contacted the Mayor regarding a possible performance there, the response was quite enthusiastic. But, they felt that the stage in their community center was not large enough to accommodate the Wind Symphony. So, unbeknownst to us, they arranged for local carpenters to build an extension that would allow for fifty, or so, musicians with chairs, music stands, instruments, and a large number of percussion instruments to fit comfortably. I remember commenting to one of our hosts that the stage was quite adequate, much more than we were expecting. Their response was something like, "Oh, no . . . the real stage is quite small. We had it enlarged just for your performance." That was when I really noticed that they had made special arrangements so that we could perform in their village. It was a magnificent gesture, and typical of the many kindnesses and courtesies that we were shown in each of our three visits to Hungary.

When we arrived, as with most of the other performance sites, we were met by the Mayor and Town Council, and given a small reception. There was a short tour of the village, and then we were taken to the performance site for a short rehearsal. After the rehearsal, there was a terrific meal . . . a sort of "pot luck" furnished by the people of the village. As always, it was an excellent meal . . . of course, all traditional Hungarian cooking. The concert that night was excellent. The house was full, with people standing in the back, and along the sides. I was reminded that we were there only a few years after the political change, and guest musicians from other countries, especially America, were still quite rare. So, our visit was a great occasion for the people of that village.

After the performance, we were invited to the "guest house" of the local winery for wine tasting . . . accompanied by various cheeses, breads, pastries, and famous Hungarian sausages. Our hosts knew that we would not partake of their wine before the concert, so they planned this special occasion for after the performance. It was excellent!

Our performance in Pécs was another grand occasion. Pécs is an ancient city founded by the Romans in the second century, in an area peopled by Celts and Pannoni tribes. The first university in Hungary was founded, in Pécs, in 1367 by Louis I, The Great. It remains the largest university in Hungary with some 34,000 students. Pécs was formed into one of the cultural and arts centers

of the country by Bishop Janus Pannonius, the great humanist poet.
Pécs is the fifth largest city in Hungary and, in 2010, was selected
to be the European Capital of Culture alongside Essen (Germany)
and Istanbul. I had visited Pécs on several occasions before this
trip, and was quite familiar with the city, and many of the local
musicians. The city hosts an excellent community band, sponsored
by the National Railway, MAV. Indeed, it is one of the finest wind
orchestras in the country.

Our return to Makó was another memorable event, very similar to
the reception we were accorded in 1996. And, our final performance
was in Budapest, hosted by the largest music school in the city. This
was to be our final tour in Hungary. We performed for large and
enthusiastic audiences in every town, city, or village in which we
appeared. We made many friends, and became quite well known
by bands and band conductors in the country. The players of the
Wind Symphony were introduced to an ancient culture, and a
musical tradition that includes several of the finest composers in
our history. Many years have passed since our visits to Hungary.
But, the warmth and hospitality of the people; the heartfelt and
generous appreciation we received, and the great adventures we
had . . . all of this is ever present in our hearts.

Italy, 2004

OUR FIRST TOUR IN ITALY was in March of 2004. Again, all of
our concert tours were scheduled during the university's spring
break ... always in the middle of March, around the occasion of
changing from Standard Time to Daylight Saving Time. Earlier,
in this section, I wrote of my aversion to taking students out of
classes. So, we always scheduled our tours for the spring break
period. Occasionally, we might leave on a Thursday or Friday,
to accommodate scheduled events of the tour. And, we always
returned on the following Friday or Saturday, to allow the students
some time to readjust, and be ready for classes starting on Monday.

Our first Italian tour was occasioned by several professional visits
to northern Italy, beginning in the spring of 2001 ... my second
sabbatical. I was invited by Maestro Lorenzo Della Fonte to be the
guest teacher for the conclusion of his year-long conducting class
in May of that year. I was also invited to appear as Guest Conductor
for the L' Orchestra di Fiati della Valtellina performance in July
at the World Association for Symphonic Bands and Ensembles
Conference in Lucerne. I made a return visit to Italy the next year,
and the following. It was from these visits that invitations for the
Wind Symphony began to surface. One of the young conductors
from Maestro Della Fonte's conducting course, Claudio Re, volunteered to make all the arrangements. The year following our tour,
Claudio enrolled as a graduate student in the School of Music at
the University of Northern Iowa, completing his Master's degree
in May of 2006. From there, he went to the University of Florida,
where he completed his Ph.D. in Musicology. After Florida, he held
conducting positions at Kenyon College (OH), Bethany College (KS),
and Cameron University (OK). He returned to his home in Italy at
the end of the fall semester in 2019.

We were in Italia from March 12 until the 20th, performing five
concerts: Manerbio (Brescia), Soresina (Cremona), Castiglione
(Mantua), Alzano Lombardo (Bergamo), and Arco (Trentino).

The program for our performances was:

Dana Wilson (USA)	*Shortcut Home* (2003)
Percy Aldridge Grainger (Australia/USA)	*Country Gardens* (1919)
	Colonial Song (1918)
	Molly on the Shore (1920)
Frigyes Hidas (Hungary)	*Capriccio* (1996)
Charles Ives (USA)	*The Alcotts* (1947)
Hardy Mertens (Netherlands)	*Xenia Sarda* (1996)
John Williams (USA)	*1941* (1979)
Eric Whitacre (USA)	*October* (2000)
Leonard Bernstein (USA)	*Suite from Candide* (1956)

Table 9: Italy 2004 tour repertoire

Dr. Rebecca Burkhardt, conductor of the Northern Iowa Symphony Orchestra, went along to help with logistics, and assist with whatever travel problems might arise. And, Chuck Pugh, Technical Director for the School of Music, along with his wife, Willie May, made the trip with us. I have included below, in italics, several comments from the students about their experiences during our journey. When we returned to Iowa, all of the students shared written memories of their experiences in Italy. As there is not room to include all of their memories, I have chosen not to name the source of the ones printed below as the messages are intended to represent all of the students.

The first concert was in Manerbio, in the province (county) of Brescia, and hosted by the Civico Corpo Bandistico "Santa Cecilia" di Manerbio. Their conductor was Arturo Andreoli, one of the finest conductors in northern Italy. Early in his career, he had been a protégé of Maestro Giovanni Ligassachi, perhaps the "godfather" of bands in northern Italy. I had met Maestro Ligassachi in the summer of 1989, when the California group, with Maestro Whitwell, performed in Brescia. Mr. Ligassachi was a master teacher and a wonderful musician/conductor. During our visit, the Maestro was quite ill. But, we were able to present, to his family, the Silver Baton Award, an award given by Kappa Kappa Psi Band Fraternity for outstanding contributions to bands and conducting. It was a great honor for us.

Figure 25: Italy 2004 tour poster

We had two days in Manerbio, and were guests of local families . . .
a great treat for the students! In the first evening, as a grand
gesture of welcome, we were given a lavish banquet, a gift from
the Manerbio band. Of course, the food was superb, a perfect
introduction to the much anticipated Italian cuisine. The entrees
were all local favorites, along with splendid *dolci* (desserts), and local
wine and grappa. Our Italian hosts easily engaged our students in
conversation, and began to establish relationships that would last
long after we returned to Iowa.

The next day, we were given a tour of the city, and were met and
welcomed by the city's Mayor and Town Council. We had a rehearsal
in the concert hall in the afternoon, followed by another wonderful
meal. The evening performance began at 9:00 PM . . . standard time
for music performances in northern Italy, and was shared with
the Manerbio band. It is tradition, in most European countries,
to exchange gifts and mementos during such events. I was able
to secure official state flags of Iowa, which had been flown above
the capitol building in Des Moines, as a gift to the city of Manerbio.
That flag was to show up at each of the next four concerts . . . more,
later! The audience was "standing room only," and wildly enthusiastic. As with our tours in Hungary, we continued our tradition
of having small chamber groups perform in the lobby before and
after the concert proper, as well as at intermission. These groups
included a trombone quartet, saxophone quartet, flute group, tuba-
euphonium quartet, and a percussion group . . . usually a theater
piece requiring techniques such as "body rhythms," drum heads,
or other unusual sounds. It was a marvelous evening, and a great
beginning to our tour.

*"I soon found out that all Italians offer the same friendship and courtesy to everyone they meet. The Italians cheered and I
cried in every venue we played in."*

The next day (a Sunday), we visited a beautiful seventeenth-century
church in Cremona, as well as Verdi's birthplace in Roncole and
his later residence (and museum) in Busetto. In the evening,
we performed at the Teatro Sociale di Soresina, a beautiful mid-

nineteenth century opera house, where the famous soprano, Renata Tebaldi, began her spectacular career. The only known "Tebaldi Fan Club" is in Soresina! The event was sponsored by the Coordinamento Banda Musicale di Cremona, an important band association in Northern Italy. As was to become the norm, the hall was filled to capacity, and very appreciative . . . we played several encores. After our opening piece, as I turned to acknowledge the applause, I noticed the Iowa flag being waved in the back of the hall . . . it was our new friends from Manerbio!

Monday was a day for visiting the sights of Verona: the famous balcony of Juliet (from Shakespeare's play), and the Colosseum (now used for opera productions in the summers) . . . and shopping! Tuesday included a tour of the city of Brescia . . . the remains of the Roman Forum there, several churches, and a piazza where Mussolini often spoke, and now the site of a terrorist bombing in 1974. We also enjoyed a lovely visit to the Museo di Santa Giulia, a large museum of archaeology, applied arts, history, and a UNESCO World Heritage Site. In the evening, we performed in another of Italy's historic opera houses, this one in the Mantova suburb of Castiglione . . . the Teatro di Castiglione della Stiviere. Our Manerbio friends showed up for that one, too!

"The emotion that I felt during and after the concerts we played was indescribable, and that feeling only fuels the passion that I have for music."

The next day, we were in Bergamo for an extended tour of the Città Alta . . . the "upper city." Bergamo occupies the site of the ancient town of Bergomum, founded in the first century AD, by the Celtic tribe of Cenomani. Beginning in the early fifteenth century, Bergamo was part of the Venetian Republic; it was the Venetians who built the stone walls around the Città Alta. Our most memorable concert of the tour was given in the Basilica di San Martino Vescovo, located in Alzano Lombardo, a suburb of Bergamo.

Our visit was made possible through the efforts of Mr. Tiziano Epis, a long time member of the Nese municipal band, a community near to Alzano Lombardo. I had met Tiziano a couple of times in previous visits, and had developed a good relationship. Along with his good friend, Roberto Vitali, also a member of the band, the two of them volunteered to loan us the necessary percussion equipment for our tour. Italian bands rarely have the needed instruments so typical of university ensembles in America … marimba, xylophone, bells, chimes, 4 timpani, etc. So, each evening, our two friends would pack the equipment in a van, drive to the town where we would perform, unload the equipment, stay for the performance, then load the equipment again, and return home. They did this five times! This was an exceptionally fine gesture, and made the tour much easier.[21]

[21] There will be more to say about Tiziano and Roberto in the account of our 2012 tour.

Our performance was part of a special Basilica concert series, and there was a full house! Beginning with our tours in Hungary, we had adopted the practice of beginning each concert with national hymns of our host country, followed by the American national anthem. That night, the entire audience stood for the playing of "The Star Spangled Banner"! At the end, as we played *Amazing Grace* for one of our encores, the audience again stood and sang or hummed along with us. It was quite a touching gesture!

With each concert, we found the Italian audiences to be quite hospitable, asking for autographs and enthusiastically congratulating our students. Many traveled far distances to attend our concerts, including musicians that I had met during previous visits. And, I met a young composer who was quite complimentary of our performance. I asked him if he had a particular favorite on the program. He replied, "Eric Whitacre's *October*." I responded that it was, indeed, a beautiful work, but wondered if there was something particular about our performance that he enjoyed. He said, "Yes … the conductor disappeared into the music!" That was one of the most touching compliments I have ever received.

"I do not think there are words to describe how wonderful this trip was!"

On Thursday, we traveled to Trento, north of the Garda Lake (Lago di Garda). Trento was the site of the Counter Reformation of the sixteenth century ... known to all music students as the "Council of Trent." Our final concert was shared with the community band from Arco di Trento, the Banda Musicale del Liceo "Antonio Rosmini" di Rovereto. We spent our last full day in the beautiful and romantic canal city of Venezia, visiting the famed Basilica di San Marco, and other historic sites. It was a wonderful finale to an unforgettable experience!

Many friendships were made during our stay in Manerbio, at the beginning of the week, with a group of thirty or so traveling to each of our concerts, and standing at the end of each performance, waving the Iowa flag. Some nights, this was a drive of two or three hours each way! It was like having our own "groupies," and a fantastic gesture of friendship and support!

This trip was planned and intended as an occasion to share our joy and passion for music-making with the people of Italy. Our hosts were exceptionally courteous and helpful, and provided first-class accommodations, terrific food (before *and* after concerts), tours of their cities and villages, and general good will. What a wonderful time ... a time "full of wonder!"

"I have never played for more receptive audiences, or experienced so much hospitality from people I had never met."

We hoped to provide a model for the bands in Northern Italy ... a model for performance repertoire, different possibilities for programming, concert etiquette, and for musical expression. Judging from the audience reaction in each venue, from newspaper reviews, and from the letters and messages from our hosts and those who heard and felt our message ... we were successful on every count! Viva Italia!

Chicago, 2008

AS NOTED EARLIER, the opening of the new Performing Arts Center in 2000 was a boon for the University and the School of Music. But, the new century also brought along some new challenges, especially with operating budgets and student recruitment. All over the nation, tuition costs had begun to rise again, making it more difficult for students to attend college. In an effort to increase the number of students coming to Northern Iowa as music majors, we thought it wise to give attention to attracting students from the states surrounding Iowa; primarily Minnesota, Illinois, and Wisconsin. Thus, for a few years, the ensembles ... Wind Symphony, Symphony Orchestra, Jazz Band I, and Concert Chorale ... elected to devote their concert tours to performing in high schools, and other venues, in those states. So, in 2008, the Wind Symphony traveled to the Chicago area for the first few days of spring break ... performing at five of the finer suburban high schools. We also visited the Chicago Art Institute; heard performances from the Chicago Symphony Orchestra and the Lyric Opera, and attended a performance of the Blue Man Group.

Italy, 2012

AFTER OUR TRIP IN 2004, I was in Italy quite often, doing guest
conducting appearances, rehearsals and clinics, and workshops
for conductors. Our tour in 2004 had been quite successful, and I
had many invitations to work with bands and conductors. So, there
were many requests for performances on this trip. We left campus
on the Thursday morning (March 8), before spring break, arriving in
Milano early Friday afternoon. For most of the players, it would be
their first European concert tour … for some, their first time on an
airplane … for all of us, a "magical mystery tour" of unforgettable
proportions! Again, I have included small remembrances from
the students. And, as before, I have not indicated the source of
the memories, wishing that they might represent the feelings and
memories of all the students.

*"I tossed and turned all night—the next morning would be the start of one of the greatest adventures that I would ever
experience. At nine o'clock in the morning I rushed over to the GBPAC to start loading the bus. For the next hour, the sixty
members of the Wind Symphony arrived to load instruments, luggage, and carry-on items onto the tour buses. Before long,
the buses were off on their way to Chicago. Little did we know, but this tour would change us in every way that we expected,
as well as every way we did not expect."*

For the first four days, we stayed in an ostello (youth hotel) in a
suburb of Bergamo … courtesy of the municipal community bands
in San Paolo d'Argon and Nese. These two bands are among the very
finest in northern Italy. We shared the first concert on Saturday
night with the San Paolo band. During the day on Saturday and
Sunday, the Wind Symphony served as the rehearsal ensemble for a
special symposium for Italian conductors. The opportunity to work
with these fine young conductors was one of the great moments of
the trip.

We performed six concerts on this trip: San Paolo d'Argon, Alzano
Lombardo, Pontevico, Brescia, Costa Volpino, and Arese.

Frigyes, Hidas (Hungary)	*Symphonic Movement* (2002)
Darius Milhaud (France)	*Suite Francaise* (1944)
Scott McAllister (USA)	*Black Dog* (2003)
Clifton Williams (USA)	*Symphonic Dance No. 3, "Fiesta"* (1965)
Charles Gonoud (France)	*"La Veau d'Or" from Faust* (1859)
Serge Rachmaninov (Russia)	*"Aleko's Cavatina" from Aleko* (1892)
Modest Mussorgsky (Russia)	*Mephistopheles' Song in Auerbach's Cellar* (1879)
David Gillingham (USA)	*Concertino for Percussion and Wind Orchestra* (1997)

Encores

Jëno Hubay (Hungary)	*Hejre, Kati* (1884)
Giuseppe Verdi (Italy)	*Infelice! . . . e tuo credevi from Ernani* (1844)
Eric Whitacre (USA)	*Seal Lullaby* (2011)

Table 10: Italy 2012 tour repertoire

"One conductor, in particular, connected with us on a level that we did not expect. When Daniela stepped onto the podium, she poured her heart out to us and we returned the favor. A tear formed in my eye as I was able to feel what she felt when she conducted. While she could not speak with us, and we could not speak with her, we understood each other . . . and that was the first of many life changing experiences for the Wind Symphony."

"The ensemble and the conductors working with us could communicate very little through spoken words, but that barrier was gone as soon as we set to making music. We had a connection we never had before, and we may never have it again. Such moments seem to escape time and space, and take us somewhere else, somewhere better . . ."

Our performance on Sunday evening was in the magnificent Basilica di San Martino in Alzano Lombardo. We had performed in this beautiful space during our 2004 tour, and were quite pleased to return. Our hosts here were the Corpo Musicale "Elia Astori" di Nese. Their conductor, Daniela Spinneli, was one of the conductors in the Conducting Symposium.

As noted earlier, I was privileged to receive a Fulbright Teaching Award for the 2004–2005 academic year, and spent the year in Pécs, Hungary, teaching at the Pécsi Tudományegyetem (University of Pécs). At Christmas time, I flew to Italy to visit friends and, again, scheduled a visit to Nese, where my friends, Tiziano Epis and Roberto Vitali, lived. I heard their New Year's Day concert, but then traveled to the northern part of the country to visit other friends in

Sondrio. I returned to Nese to have a nice dinner with Tiziano and
Roberto, and other members of the band. I was to change trains
in Lecco, but somehow the connecting train was late, or I was late
getting to Lecco. In any case, I had a cell phone with me, and called
Tiziano to say that I would be late in arriving. He indicated that he
was a bit ill, and would not be able to come for the dinner, but would
try to see me before I left Italy. I was a bit distraught at being late,
and expressed my disappointment at not being able to see him. He
said, "Don't worry, Ronald. Everything will be okay." Those turned
out to be his last words to me, as he died a few days later ... after
I had returned to Hungary. His illness was, in fact, a quite serious
lung condition, though I am not aware of the specifics.

I was able to return to Italy again at the close of my time in Hungary,
and before returning to Iowa. I scheduled a time to visit with the
band in Nese, and visited Tiziano's burial site. After that, I returned
to work with the band each time I was in Italy, which was almost
every year for a while. Roberto and I became very good friends,
and were in contact regularly. The relationship with the Nese band,
and with Roberto became closer each time we were together, and I
have so many beautiful memories of our friendship. When it came
time to start planning for the 2012 tour, I knew that we should
perform again in the Alzano Lombardo Basilica. And, of course,
Roberto and the band arranged for that to happen. (As it turned
out, our performance was the last concert of non-religious music
heard in the Basilica.) In planning repertoire, I wanted to perform
something special for Tiziano during that concert. I chose Eric
Whitacre's *Seal Lullaby*, and we performed it as an encore ... the
final piece of the evening. Before we played, I said some words
about Tiziano ... how I had met him; how he and Roberto had
helped us in 2004. Tiziano's parents were in the audience, as was
the entire Nese band. Our performance was quite emotional, the
players were quite taken with Tiziano's story. When the music was
finished, the players and the audience ... and, me ... were in tears.

"The church itself was beautiful, but the performance of the Wind Symphony made the experience complete. A tearful encore in memory of Tiziano Epis, a close friend of Dr. Johnson and the Wind Symphony, ended our concert on an unforgettable note."

Monday was a "free day," the only one in which we did not perform. Our hosts took us on a walking tour of the Città Alta, the old "upper" part of the city of Bergamo. In the afternoon and evening, everyone was free to discover if they were truly prepared to negotiate the Italian restaurants and shops.

"We found a little restaurant in a back alley that served us a three course meal for ten Euros. The food was indescribable. The tastes were real, no additives, and I could actually enjoy the meal . . . selected by the waiter at our request. It consisted of pea soup, pasta, salad, and a meat dish . . . which none of us know the name of to this day."

On Tuesday morning, we traveled to Cremona, one of the great cities of the Renaissance, and home to some two hundred violin makers. In the evening, we were in Pontevico, a lovely small community south of Brescia. The concert was, again, hosted and sponsored by the town band, and organized by their conductor, Giorgio Zanolini. The performance was held in the city's newly renovated theater, and was filled to capacity. The students were overcome by the kindness and generosity of our Italian host families . . . everyone quickly developing new relationships, sharing email and Facebook addresses—making promises to return.

"Pontevico is a small town, but when we got there, it was our largest reception. After our tour of the city and the only blacksmith shop left in Northern Italy, we put on a concert that was packed—the whole town came for our concert! Afterwards, a buffet-style feast with the local youth band and our hosts . . . who, for the most part, did not speak English!"

"After the concert, we went with Costantino and his wife Giulia back to their home for a more private dinner. Needless to say, the food they served was absolutely fantastic, from the meal itself to the cheese and wine afterward. But, the best part was the conversation. Costantino himself spoke a fair bit of English but not a lot, and his wife spoke next to none. We spoke no Italian. But regardless of those facts, we talked for hours into the night. But of everything we spoke of, most important was a promise I made to return one day. And I will."

After a tearful farewell to our Pontevico family hosts and friends on Wednesday morning, we headed north for Brescia, one of the great cities of northern Italy, and one of the best sites for exploring ancient ruins from the Roman period. The day was given to a tour

of the city and the Roman ruins. Our concert was jointly hosted
by the Brescia municipal government and the Luca Marenzio
Conservatory of Music, and held in the PalaBrescia, the largest
concert hall in Brescia. In the evening, the Wind Symphony was
presented with an honorary diploma from the Conservatory, a
very special honor! As Italian tradition dictates, all of our concerts
started at 9:00 PM (21:00!), usually with a dinner or some sort of
reception afterwards. This made for long days and short sleep!!
We were again with host families in Brescia, much appreciated by
everyone. The opportunity to be in Italian homes, eat Italian food,
speak the Italian language (usually poorly) ... to discover that we
are much more alike than we are different ... this was the great gift
from our hosts.

"Performing for the gracious audiences of several great communities in Italy truly hit home the idea that music is the universal language. Through music, I was able to communicate with many I will never see again, yet I know that their lives are as changed as my own."

On Thursday morning, we traveled to the beautiful village of
Sermione, located on a small peninsula jutting out from the south
shore of the Garda Lake. Sermione was a resort of sorts during
the Roman period, and has remained so to the present day. Our
Brescia organizer, Renato Krug, arranged for a local historian to
take us on a short tour of the area. The rest of the day was given
to exploring, shopping, sitting by the lake, and practicing our language skills with the waiters at local restaurants. In the evening,
we performed in Costa Volpino, another lake community ... this
one on the northern end of Lake Iseo. Our concert was, again, performed in a beautiful church, and organized by another of the fine
conductors we worked with, Giuseppe Martinelli. The lake was
especially beautiful in the late evening and early morning ... one of
our favorite memories!

"And, from my friends, I learned how to love one another, especially in new situations and places, and that was a really great learning experience for me."

"This truly was a life-changing experience, and one that I'm so grateful to have been a part of!"

On Friday morning, we loaded the buses and headed for Milano . . .
our last day in Italia! Our host was Luca Pasqua, Music Director of
Vox Aurea, a community music association in the town of Arese,
a suburb of Milano. We were given a tour of the museum at the
La Scala Opera House, a memorable treat for musicians. And, we
visited the Duomo di Milano, the fourth largest cathedral in the
world . . . WOW! In the evening, we performed our final concert, the
program shared with the Vox Aurea band. There was a terrific meal
for us afterward, our last taste of Italian cuisine. It was fabulous . . .
as were they all!

Figure 26: Italy 2012 concert poster

*"Lets compare: in one instance, an Italian waiter and myself were completely
baffled at how to complete a transaction with each other. In another, an
audience reacted with such exuberance and gusto to our performance. There
were shouts of "Bravi!," and no confusion over what just transpired and
how to react. Music and the arts speak to the soul without hesitation and
question. As artists, we can never forget this notion; it is our universal
mission."*

On Saturday morning, after a few hours sleep, we arrived at the
Milano Malpensa airport around 6:30 AM . . . the return flight left
at 9:30 AM. We arrived in Chicago around 5:00 PM, collected our
luggage and instruments, and loaded the buses (for the last time!)
for the trip back to Cedar Falls. We arrived around 11:00 PM . . . tired,
but happy to be home.

*"Our trip to Italy was a wonderful string of favorite moments. For me, the best part about this trip was the experience of
enjoying these moments with the people around me. While my eyes were being opened to new truths about the nature
of music and community, the friend next to me was learning the same thing. While I gazed in wonder at magnificent
cathedrals, the friend next to me was also craning her neck to see the same thing. While I savored each wonderful bite of a
new pasta masterpiece, the friend next to me was also exploring whole new worlds of culinary depth. Italy allowed us to look
around and see a whole group of changed people blooming together."*

We had been aware, almost from the first moment, that we were
all part of an incredible journey, one that would change us in so
many ways. Now, back home, we would begin to feel . . . quite

deeply ... how we were different. The change would only become more pronounced and intensely felt in the days and weeks to come. We went to Italy to share our music with Italian audiences. We believed that the power of great music can change people's lives and heal the soul. We were also keen to represent well the traditions and values of the School of Music and the University, the State of Iowa, and America. What we received in return was something of magic and wonder ... an opening of our hearts that has allowed us to know more of the world ... and ourselves.

"After having spent a week in a foreign country with such great people, playing such great music, of course I have become a different person."

"I really loved how the Italians were so friendly and excited to listen to us play, or to host us in their homes. I learned a lot from the Italians about how to appreciate and really love music."

As one might imagine, a trip such as this would not have been possible without the support and encouragement of many people. With the state of the economy at the time, and the fact that prices seemed to change regularly, it is no small miracle that we were able to make this all happen. Caroline Francis, Administrative Assistant for the School of Music acted as "tour manager" ... handling schedules, taking care of correspondence, dealing with the airline folks and the University Business Office, getting the bills paid, saving all of us from many difficulties and obstacles ... we absolutely could not have done it without her! John Hines (bass) and Amanda McCandless (clarinet), members of our Artist Faculty, went along as soloists. Their superb musicianship earned them standing ovations every night. And, their good will and exceptional "tour chops" made them a real joy to have around. Dr. Rebecca Burkhardt, Conductor of the Northern Iowa Symphony Orchestra, went along as part of the teaching faculty for the conducting seminar at the beginning of the tour, as well as spiritual mentor for us all. Keith Kennedy, from our Media Production Services, went along as our "official" photographer and filmmaker. His professionalism and unflagging good will was a huge help! [22] And, I gratefully acknowledge the enthusiastic

[22] One can find the video of our 2012 tour on YouTube ... entitled *Bravi!: The Italian Tour.*

support and good will of the School of Music Faculty. Without their professionalism, ongoing commitment to high standards, and willingness to assist the students in their preparation, we could not have made this trip!

The Italians . . . aaah! The Italians! The one person who made it all work was Denis Salvini, conductor, teacher, and horn player in the Bergamo/Brescia area, and long-time friend. Denis arranged for all of the concerts, made arrangements with the bus company, organized the conducting seminar, made arrangements for the use of the larger instruments that we could not bring with us, and took care of whatever problems arose each day. Denis is a "force for good" in northern Italy . . . he is a great conductor and musician, a trusted friend and colleague for us all. Helping Denis with the details was Roberto Vitali, our good friend and colleague with the band in Nese. At each concert site, the bands and their conductors . . . the city councils, the family hosts, the audience members . . . all were genuinely pleased to have us in their community, and did all they could to make our visit one to be remembered.

The real heroes of this "Great Italian Romp" were, of course, the students. As their conductor, I felt privileged each day to be part of this extraordinary group of human beings. Tours such as this take a mighty toll on the body and the spirit. Not once did I hear complaints . . . they became a family. They cared for each other's needs when someone was ill, and offered an understanding shoulder to lean on when spirits sagged. Though their bodies were often tired and weak, their belief in our cause never faltered. They believed that every concert was an opportunity to change people's hearts and minds. And, every night, they were successful in that belief. Every concert was a remarkable experience . . . for us, as well as the listeners. Every night there were moments that we will remember for the remainder of our lives. Every night offered a new lesson in what it means to be human. Even the Italians were proud of them. I could see it in the eyes of their host families as we left in the morning . . . the way they tearfully hugged each other, not wanting to let go. I could see it in the eyes of the Italian musicians and audience members as they rushed to congratulate them after concerts. No one who was part of this journey . . . neither the students nor the faculty . . . not the Italian audiences or the host families . . . will soon forget this exceptional group of young people. Bravissimo!

"Since being back, you can see the light in everyone's eyes. You can see the change it made in our hearts. You can see the love that we experienced and gave. There is a sort of gentleness in the air—a relaxed atmosphere. There is an unspoken understanding between the sixty of us—we know what we experienced and we feel it every single day. The love is there, the compassion is there, and all woes and worries have long since passed. We are different people now because we chose to be a part of something bigger. We chose to give of ourselves and that led us down a "road less traveled", as Robert Frost wrote, "and that has made all the difference."

Figure 27: Italy 2012, Northern Iowa Wind Symphony performing in the Basilica di San Martino Vescovo in Alzano Lombardo

Italy, 2016, "The Warrior Tour"

AS INDICATED EARLIER, I formally retired from the university at the end of the spring semester of 2016, but remained for the following academic year, only conducting the Wind Symphony. My retirement was announced in January of 2016, with the intent of allowing sufficient time for the university to search for my successor. So, the students knew that this would be our final tour together and I believe that they, as well as myself, knew that it would be a special one.

As was our custom with previous tours, we began preparing in the fall semester. I programmed a few pieces from the tour program on the two fall concerts, and on the February (band festival) concert. All through the fall semester, we talked about the tour in the spring ... about previous tours, about Italian culture, about travel expectations, about all of it. Near the end of the fall, we met on a couple of evenings to talk about important facets of the tour. In the spring, we had a few more meetings in the evening. As one might imagine, preparing for a trip such as this requires extensive planning. I especially wanted the students to have as much information as possible in order for them to feel comfortable and secure in what should happen ... or *might* happen ... when we got to Italy.

THROUGHOUT THE FALL SEMESTER, we had some difficulty in finding our "center" ... our Soul. After some forty-five years of university teaching, I had learned that each year was different ... that traditions and customs continued, but each year brought a unique set of circumstances. This particular year, the students ... as well as much of the faculty ... experienced a degree of unease that was difficult to identify, but was surely felt by all of us. So, we made a few small changes to address our unease. The first change was that we took the first few minutes of each rehearsal for students to speak about whatever was on their mind. On Mondays, anyone could announce whatever new or exciting thing was happening in their lives ... acceptance to graduate school, good grade on an exam, announcement of an upcoming recital, etc. On Wednesdays, we reserved time for asking for help with some particular problem they might be experiencing ... difficult course outside the School of Music, problem with a non-music major roommate, some family issue at home, etc. This seemed to allow the students the occasion to air some of their angst and frustrations. And, of course, once their fellow players were aware of the issues, they were more than willing to help each other in finding solutions, and easing the situation. We agreed that whatever was said in the rehearsal room ... that it *stayed* in the room. An enormous trust began to develop among the players. For two hours on Mondays and Wednesdays, Davis Hall became a refuge, a place of safety ... it became sacred for us.

The excellent Brazilian writer, Paulo Coelho, has long been a favorite of mine, having read several of his books, including his most famous one, *The Alchemist.* In the summer before this academic year, I had read his *Warrior of the Light,* and found it quite helpful ... a book which spoke to the issues of the courage and fortitude needed to stand in the face of Life's obstacles and disappointments. I bought nine copies, and gave one to each of the section Principals. They, in turn, passed it around their section for each player to read. It is a relatively short book, one can easily read it in a single evening. The students seemed to enjoy the book very much, and began to talk about it among themselves, or to read a favored passage to the group at the beginning of rehearsals. As time went by, and our departure for Italy came closer, several students began to refer to our upcoming journey as "The Warrior Tour." It was an apt title.

Another practice, which we had developed for those years in which we were scheduled for a tour, was to use the Friday and Saturday before the beginning of spring classes as a time for concentrated rehearsal and discussion. For this year's occasion, we had a "community meal" on Friday evening following the afternoon rehearsal. From the players, I gathered eight or nine crock pots, and spent the previous day preparing my secret recipe for "Johnson's Killer Chili" ... enough for everyone. The players brought salads, desserts, chips and dip, soft drinks, and water. We had some problems getting all of the crock pots to work properly, due to "dead" electrical outlets, but we made it work. After the meal, we watched a movie in one of the large rooms in the PAC with a big screen TV. It was a great evening!

It was during this weekend that we developed our *Credo*, a statement of what we believed, and what we intended to represent.

The Wind Symphony Credo

This is what we believe; this is who we are

We aspire to the highest expressions of Being
… in performance; in scholarship; in leadership

We believe that music can heal the Soul's wounds …
and ease suffering of the Spirit

We are not distracted by unattainable efforts toward perfection.
Rather, we direct our attention to the discovery of the
highest levels of expression that lie within each of us

We are invested in community … seeking transformative experiences
which support the interconnectedness among
composers, performers, and listeners

We choose to be responsible for each other …
and, to each other

For the tasks given to us, it shall always be our intention
to give the best of which we are capable

In the weeks which followed, indeed for the remainder of the year and especially during the tour, this *Credo* became a means of binding us together, of helping us to find our "center" … we started to belong to one another.

I invited Robert Washut and Anthony Williams to come along with us as soloists. Dr. Washut had composed a piece a couple of years earlier, especially for the Wind Symphony with solo piano. And, Dr. Williams had been a graduate student at the time of our first Italian tour in 2004. Now, he had returned and was a member of our Artist Faculty.

What follows is an account of the tour taken from an article appearing in the Fall 2016 edition of *Rhythms*, the annual news magazine from the School of Music. Five of our senior level students did most of the writing; I did most of the editing. And, it has been further

edited for this accounting. Those students were Linnea Casey, Stacia Fortune, Brent Mead, Lucas Petersen, and Nicholas Schumacher.
And, once more, I have retained the practice of not naming the
source of the quotes. The written memories of the students were
quite emotional, expressive, and numerous. My intention was to
select the memories which spoke for all of us.

The program was:

John Williams (USA)	*Summon the Heroes* (1996)
Frank Gulino (USA)	*Capriccio for Solo Trombone and Wind Ensemble* (2010)
John Frantzen (USA)	*Poem* (1998)
William Connor (England)	*Tails aus dem Vood Viennoise* (1993)
Robert Washut (USA)	*The High Road* (2013)
Julie Giroux (USA)	*Culloden* (2000)

Encores
Rolf Rudin (Germany)	*Amen* (2013)
John Mackey (USA)	*Sheltering Sky* (2012)

Table 11: Italy 2016 tour repertoire

"Each night that we performed, I looked around at the ensemble differently. I not only saw the faces of friends, but faces of individual people fighting their own struggles, hardships and battles. Some of the performances themselves brought challenges; both logistically and mentally. The exhaustion of traveling and performing almost every night was a difficult challenge to overcome, but each night we made it happen. We performed some of the most beautiful music I've ever heard from this ensemble. These performances, months later now, are still in my dreams and give me chills. This trip was an experience I will never forget."

On Thursday, March 10, we left Cedar Falls at 5:30 AM and headed to
Chicago, O'Hare. From there, we flew to Newark, New Jersey, and at
6:35 PM said goodbye to America (and normal phone service!). Most
of us had never been to another country; a few had never been on an
airplane, and some had never before left Iowa! We arrived in Milano,
Italy at 8:00 AM on Friday, March 11, and our "Warrior Tour" began.

"My favorite memory of the week was all the unexpected friendships that were made with members of this group and the Italians. Music has the ability to break down whatever barriers that may separate us, and helps us to express ourselves in our true forms. The sights were great but the music that we shared is what I will remember forever."

At Milano Malpensa airport, we met Maestro Denis Salvini, our great friend and tour manager for the week, and began our first day of great adventure. We traveled to the small village of Roncole: the birthplace of Giuseppe Verdi. We visited a small museum commemorating the art and literature of Giovanni Guareschi, a famous Italian cartoonist and author. We then enjoyed an elaborate multi-course meal at the Trattoria Le Roncole, complete with homemade pasta, salads, cured meats, delicious cheeses, espresso, gelato, good conversation and high hopes for the week to come. After this wonderful introduction to Italia, we explored the small village and visited the church where Verdi played organ and piano as a young man: the Chiesa di San Michele Arcangelo (the church of Saint Michael, the Archangel). Then, we drove to Busetto to visit some other historical sites of Verdi: an outdoor opera theatre and a statue in his memory. From there, we traveled to Palazzolo Sull'Oglio, where we were honored with a welcome ceremony from the Mayor of the city, and then dinner at Restaurante Capri. After dinner, we had our first solid sleep in almost forty hours.

Figure 28: Italy 2016 tour, UNIWS at Verdi's birthplace

On Saturday and Sunday, we served as the ensemble for a conducting seminar for Italian conductors (and, one from Greece!). We also had tours of Palazzolo and some free time on both days. Many of us were positively and powerfully impacted by the visible changes in the conductors who were able to work with us. For some, this was one of the most transformative experiences of the week.

"My favorite memory was when Marta (one of the Italian conductors) started crying during the conducting seminar. It not only sparked a change in her heart, but you could see every single person in the room was moved by the experience. We made such beautiful music and it changed her life by knowing how she can see and feel the music being made with her eyes shut. This helped me appreciate being a part of this group and knowing that we are capable of changing lives in everything we do."

On Saturday evening, we performed in the concert space where we had spent the day. Performing in our chamber groups for the first time (saxophones, brass quintet, trombones, tuba/euphonium, flute, percussion) for this huge audience was an especially exhilarating experience. On Sunday, after the seminar, we traveled to the town of Leno, where our hosts honored us with a welcome tour of the highlights of the city and had a visit with the Mayor of the village. Generously, they gave us a reception before and after the concert. The Italian pastries and refreshments were fresh and delicious, to say the least. For the concert that night, we shared the program with the municipal band of Leno, the Corpo Musicale Lenese: Vincenzo Capirola.

Figure 29: Italy 2016 tour, the American and Italian national flags for our performance in Leno

"I loved all of the performances . . . the music we produced was so raw and pure, I would become sad after every performance because I knew that I would never experience anything like this again."

Monday was a day full of sightseeing in the beautiful city of Shakespearean fame: Verona. We were able to wander freely, enjoying Italian clothing and shoe stores, beautiful ancient architecture, churches and delicious meals for most of the day before heading to the next concert in Soresina, a village near to Cremona. That night, we performed in the Teatro Sociale di Soresina, a beautiful nineteenth-century opera house, a place where we had performed during the 2004 tour. This was a particularly emotional concert for us, as we had all been in constant motion and working since our arrival in Italy. After an exhausting first half, we gained a rush of energy and performed the most invested second half yet. By the end of the night, we were revitalized to continue forging through the week.

As a consequence of all the previous tours, I had learned a lot about what happens to students, and their physical bodies, when they experience such dramatic changes as those which occur during tours in another country. Everything is new and different. Different time zone, different food, different language, customs, culture . . . all of it. Most students are already tired and depleted when the tour starts . . . tired from the demands of the academic world, and from the heavy schedule of rehearsals, classes, and performances. So, it is not unusual for students to become ill during tours. I always encouraged them to bring along medications for colds and flu, as well as vitamin supplements to support the increased demands on their bodies. And, I learned that regardless of how much information they are given, there will still be some confusion and self-doubt.

So, we added the practice of gathering together after concerts, or anytime that we would separate from each other. We gave our gatherings the name, "huddle." And each night, after the performance, we would gather behind the stage or other acceptable space, and discuss what comes next. I would stand in the center, and the players would gather around me . . . we stood close, as a family. I would ask if anyone was ill, if they needed medication of some sort. Were there problems of any sort? Did anyone need anything? We also took the occasion to speak about the performance just concluded. Each night was a huge expenditure of emotion and feeling . . . they needed to share that with each other. The "huddle" was our "safe place," a place for the family to connect before being separated for the night. This became one of the highlights of our trip. I was astonished at the outpouring of love and support that they gave each time. Looking back at the other tours, I wondered how much our huddling would have added to those tours.

"I learned something important on this trip: when one is part of a family, they must rise up to the challenges in front of them for the sake of the family. There was a point in Soresina where I decided I wasn't going to let my insecurities cripple the group. I came into the second half of that concert ready to give everything I had for the sake of the group. I grew as a musician and person because I was able to see that people believed in me. At that point, there was no desire to wallow in my own doubt and self-pity. I was able to play to the best of my ability and I had a wonderful time and I hope I had half the impact on you all that you had on me. Thank you for inspiring me to grow up. I will cherish the memories we made this week for the rest of my life. I love you all."

On Tuesday, we departed from Soresina and traveled to the Aosta Valley where we had an opportunity to see the sights and do some shopping. After a morning full of touring, friends and food, we met up again to head to our next concert site at Nus, a suburb of Aosta. After another beautiful concert with great acoustics, we stayed the night with host families. This was the first night for many of us to meet an Italian family and spend time in their home. What a treat!

"While it is virtually impossible to come up with one favorite memory or moment, one that really stands out was playing 'Sheltering Sky' at our concert in Nus. From the very first note of the piece, I was overcome by how beautiful it was. I was so grateful that we were all together, creating amazing music, that I cried more than I have in recent memory. When we finished the piece, I was stunned that we had just created the most awe-inspiring, incredible musical experience that I have been, and probably ever will be, a part of."

On Wednesday, we finally reached our "free day". No concert to prepare for that evening helped relax the atmosphere in the group, and we all took a much needed mental break. We began the day with a visit to a castle at the entrance of the Aosta Valley, named the Bard Fortress. This has been the site of various degrees of military fortification since the fifth century. This castle is now a museum and houses an art gallery and a photography exhibit as well as an exhibit detailing the history of the castle itself. After a nice lunch at a restaurant (inside the castle!), we traveled to Verbania for our last two days of great adventure. We first checked in at the hostel before the evening activities. Ready for adventure, we all wandered the beautiful streets of Verbania to find the best restaurants and quality establishments that the city had to offer. With all the challenges we surmounted in the first few days, going out in the dark, cold night (it had snowed that morning) to navigate a new city seemed a fairly simple task.

Figure 30: Italy 2016 tour, Forte di Bard (Bard Fortress)

"The tour in Italy was definitely filled with ups and downs for all of us. We had difficulties with scheduling, accommodations and many of us were always tired. Despite all of that, I am impressed with each member of this ensemble for stepping up to the plate and giving 100% at every single concert. I saw genuine happiness in people from whom I had not seen a sincere smile in months. I heard laughter, saw all of the companionship and bonds that were being formed, and felt warmth in my heart. You are all wonderful, beautiful people, and being with you in Italy meant the world to me."

On Thursday, we would perform our last concert . . . for which we felt both excited and reluctant, because it meant the week would soon be over. We spent the time before the concert enjoying Verbania with its gorgeous view of Lago Maggiore and the surrounding Alps. Some of us had picnics, bathing in the sunlight, while others perused the artisan-owned shops in the town (with many finding Italian leather shoes and handbags!). After a nice day of exploring the city, we reconvened one last time for a concert in the church of Madonna di Campagna (Our Lady of the Country). We knew that this would be the last concert tour for Dr. Johnson, so many of us felt strong emotions and a sense of reverence for this performance. Adding to this effect was the venue itself; the church contained ancient frescoes, a bell tower, and wood architecture all dating back to the sixteenth century. The stone walls created a very resonant space for our music and we all felt very blessed to be there, living entirely in that moment.

Figure 31: Italy 2016 tour, Chiesa di
Madonna di Campagna

"You all have shown me that we are capable of creating something incredibly powerful, healing and beautiful. There was a man in the audience in Verbania who sat on the edge of his seat for the entire concert. I feel like I saw him be changed and encouraged through our music. That experience changed me. I'm going to keep pursuing music and have fun doing it. It feels like a gift to have this joy for music and I want to thank you all for that."

"My favorite part of the trip musically was the concert in Verbania. I loved how Dr. Johnson told us that this we were doing this last concert for us. I usually go through concerts trying to get through it and don't take the time to actually enjoy the music that our group is producing. I decided to listen to and enjoy the music at this final concert. Between the fact that our music was absolutely beautiful and that we were in such a sacred place as that beautiful church made that moment very meaningful. I am very proud to be in such an amazing group as the Wind Symphony! Both because it is made up of wonderful people and because we can do great things when we all come together with our music!"

We left Verbania at 5:30 AM on Friday morning, traveling to Milano for the return flights to America . . . arriving in Cedar Falls around midnight.

"My experience of the tour was way beyond what I expected . . . the kindness of the people, the flavorful cuisine, the breathtaking landscapes, the ancient architecture and the appreciation of our music exceeded anything I had imagined. On about day four in Verona, I had a great conversation with friends about the cultural differences of Italy compared to the USA . . . not the least of which were the attitudes about food, friends, and music. Italians love to lengthen the experience of all three— savoring each moment with considerable pleasure. I now wish so earnestly that more Americans could have this experience. We could all use a little more, 'più ancora', of the Italian philosophy in our daily interactions with each other.

In a musical respect, this trip could scarcely have been more rewarding. It was our goal to deliver a magnificent performance with technical excellence and emotional subtlety every night, and to heal the hearts and minds of audiences we played for. With gratitude, I can say our goal was immensely supported by our audience of rapt listeners every night that we performed. Their reception was so generous and the encores kept coming, to my astonishment. Their non-verbal communication conveyed that we had accomplished our goal, and I especially hope that their hearts were touched as much as it showed on their faces.

Performing at such a high level every night took great spiritual and physical endurance, especially after long days of touring cities and riding buses. Despite all of the struggles and unexpected snags along the way, the greatest comfort to me was knowing that each night I would be surrounded by my friends and our trusted conductor to share our art with anyone who came to receive it. At our concerts, the language barrier was not a problem; personally, I realized even if I have difficulty describing a feeling that I get from music, it can emote for itself to the listener whatever they need most at that moment.

Even though each venue was different, from the intimate, surprisingly dry Soresina opera house to the resonant Chiesa di Madonna di Campagna, we made adjustments and played our hearts out every night. With each beat of the music, and our hearts, our fondness for Italy and each other grew stronger. It pains me to be graduating this year and leaving this ensemble behind. And I think we all want to return to Italy someday. However, I have faith that the legacy of the Wind Symphony will continue. Even though I'll no longer play with them, I can still return to listen and recall precious times together and bonds formed."

This final tour was something very special for all of us. There were changes and challenges every day, and the students handled it all with grace and professionalism. As a matter of fact, there were many times when paid professionals would not have been able to rise to the occasion. I was always proud of our students when we were away from home, on tour. But, this group had something special. One can read in their memories of their commitment, and of their courage. I think it not important that the reader know precisely of the difficulties and challenges they encountered. What *is* important, I think, is to know that they summoned the courage, and the bravery, to overcome those obstacles. And, one can feel that in their words. They became Warriors!

"The term "Warrior Tour" fits this trip perfectly. Every person involved became a warrior during or after the trip based on the experiences we all underwent throughout the week. Perseverance, compassion and patience became our core values as plans changed and tensions grew. But in the end, I believe we came out as a stronger, more whole, family of musicians and friends."

In the final few years of my tenure, it became custom for me to send a final message to the players ... congratulating them on the season just ended and, perhaps, indicating plans for the coming year. This year, I wrote the following letter.

Fellow Warriors,

Before we get too far into the summer ... and the memories of the past year recede further into our consciousness ... I wanted to express my appreciation to all of you, and say farewell to those who are leaving us. As you have so often heard me complain ... we live in a time, and in a society, in which we rarely take time to reflect on the nature and direction of our lives, or those who have helped us get this far. We fill our lives with so much activity, so much busy-ness ... that we quite easily can lose touch with our core human values, those meaningful expressions of our soul, those feelings and emotions we hold as artists. I hope that you will take time to do that now, while memories are still close.

There is an expression which comes from our own American Civil War . . . "All gave some; some gave all." Let us remember, and be thankful for, those who gave something more . . . who committed to serve and support. Among these are our Principal Players . . . arranging for section rehearsals; communicating with me about mutual concerns; communicating with each other; creating teamwork and cooperation within the sections . . . this helped us to become who we are. Remember, and be thankful for, their willingness to assume the mantle of leadership . . . their love for you, and their commitment to the Wind Symphony.

There were those who committed to creating, and putting into action, our PawPrints video campaign. Their efforts helped us to make possible many parts of the tour that, otherwise, would not have been possible (Le Roncole). Much appreciation to them!

Thanks to Joe for arriving early before every rehearsal to arrange the chairs and stands for you. Joe can tell you that I can be quite particular about where each chair is placed. Joe showed up every day and endured my peculiarities with smiles and good will. He listened to my complaints about lighting in Davis; took care of the piano (including Dr. Washut's electric piano), and took care of whatever other things were needed to prepare for your arrival to each rehearsal. Bravo, Joe!

Thanks to Alex and the percussion team. While the rest of us could show up a few minutes before rehearsal and be fine, the percussionists had to arrive a half hour before . . . to arrange for multiple mallet instruments, multiple drums, cymbals, timpani, and a myriad of "little stuff." And, when everyone else left at the end of rehearsal, they stayed longer and put away all of that equipment. Thanks, Alex, Michael, Megan, Patrick, and Nick (and, Kyler). And, thanks to the fluties for becoming their friends in Italy!!

I have attached a copy of the story of our "Warrior Tour." A shortened version will appear in the fall issue of *Rhythms*, the annual magazine of the School of Music. And, it will be posted on the SOM website, replacing the story of our 2012 Tour. Thanks to Linnea, Stacia, Brent, Nick, and Lucas for their work in creating this wonderful story of love and adventure. And, I have attached links to the five pieces from our April concert. I think you will be pleased with our efforts. Please share these with all your friends and family.

We had an amazing year together. At this time a year ago, who among us would have imagined the unforgettable journey we would travel together. We were fifty individuals, looking for the path to meld into a single entity . . . a force for goodness forged from our own dreams and struggles. From rehearsals to performances, and back to rehearsals, we found our way. We were not without setbacks and missteps, disappointments and sadness. But, we kept getting up each day, summoning the courage to try and make today better than yesterday. Slowly, we became Warriors . . . we became vigilant, for our Selves and for each other . . . we became a family. We shared an experience that will be remembered only by us . . . only we precious few. While our "band of brothers and sisters" will never be together again, we will always have our memories of being together . . . those memories of shining moments, however brief they may have been, that offered us an insight into the greatness which lives in each of us; our vision of purpose and commitment. You will always have that. Let it become a source of inspiration for your future.   For those who will return in the fall . . . I hope that you will be able to reflect on the year just ended, and allow the growth and transformation you achieved to become the foundation for the continuing evolution of your mind and soul. The next year can be even more adventuresome and life-altering than was this one. It will be, as it has always been, your choice. Choose wisely! For those who are leaving us . . . please know that you are loved, and will be missed. We were different because you were with us, and we will be different because you are gone from us.

I am forever changed because of you. The struggles we shared; the moments of exhilaration we created; the love we found . . . I am transformed by all of that. I am pleased that you allowed me to be part of your life's journey . . . I am happy that you were part of mine.

Take care of each other . . . keep close.

rjohnson

Figure 32: Italy 2016 tour, Northern Iowa Wind Symphony in the Teatro Sociale di Soresina

Coda

WHEN I FIRST ARRIVED on the campus of the University of Northern Iowa in the fall of 1982, I could not have imagined that we would be able to accomplish all that we did. In the beginning, I knew I wanted to have a great ensemble. I knew I wanted to perform great music. I knew I wanted to create an arena in which students could come to love music as much as I did. And, I knew I wanted our music-making to touch the hearts and souls of the people who heard us, and change their lives. Beyond that, I really could not imagine much. As with all journeys, we cannot truly "see" what comes next until we move to that level. While we can have a clear vision . . . or, at least, what we think is clear . . . of where we have been, the road ahead is almost always unknown, always a challenge. It seems that the most we can really hope to do is prepare, as best we can, for whatever comes next.

For a while, one of my most fervent dreams was to have a position at a famous university where I imagined there would only be good students, and everything worked exactly as it should. Of course, not only does that place *not* exist, but . . . if it *had* existed . . . it would have deprived me of the opportunity for real growth, for facing problems and difficulties, searching for solutions, and getting better. And, I would have missed the experience of working and making music with some of the finest young men and women anywhere in the world. An ancient Chinese proverb says, "the journey of a thousand miles begins with a single step." Yes! Correct! It does! We have to start where we are, and begin the journey.

The more we travel, the more clearly can we see *where* we want
to go. Our path comes to be more focused, we begin to notice
more. We encounter many crossroads and "roads less traveled."
Slowly, we come to understand that, with life-journeys, there is no
destination ... there is only *journey*. And, as the journey continues,
it reveals more of who we are, who we want to be, and what we wish
to represent.

The things we ... WE, the Wind Symphony and my Self ... were
able to achieve were a consequence of the ever present need, and
desire, to get better ... to know and understand more, to feel more,
to contribute more, to be more. Sometimes, we were not successful
in our efforts. Sometimes, things did not go as we hoped for. What
we learned to do was to examine our failures and missteps, make
adjustments, and try again. The key was always to keep focused
on the goal, and learn to make changes which supported that goal.
Early on, I learned that students almost never did what I said to do.
But, they almost always did what I did. That was a heady discovery.
It meant that if I wanted excellence from the students, I first had
to find excellence within my Self. If I wanted them to get better, I
had to get better first. As Mahatma Gandhi observed, "One must
become the change they want to see in the world."

Of course, none of what we were able to achieve would have been
possible without the support and encouragement of many other
people. We were helped by an excellent faculty in the university's
School of Music. There are many generations of UNI graduates who
enjoy successful careers in performance and education because of
the great teaching from that faculty. There were three Directors
of the School of Music during my tenure, and each of them was
a strong advocate for the Wind Symphony ... indeed, for all of
the ensembles. Since the 1980s, university funding has always
been problematic, more so in recent years ... there simply is not
enough money to do what needs to be done for the students, and
the mission of the university. Still, the University Administration
was able to find support, sometimes from outside sources, for each
of our international tours ... experiences that changed our lives
forever.

The world has changed now ... everything is different. As I write this, we are still in the midst of a global pandemic that cannot seem to find a solution. The political situation in America is, perhaps, at its most divisive point in our nation's history. The world's climate continues to change and create disasters, a consequence of our inability ... or, our refusal ... to take care of our planet. People are tired, frustrated, and fearful for what may happen in the future. Whatever that future might be, we will never again be as we were. When I first started to write this about a year and a half ago, I only wanted to record the "data" of what happened ... the repertoire we performed, the European tours, the basics of what we did together. But, as time went by, I came to realize that the conditions in which we lived, the opportunities that were available to us at the time, and the *ethos* of our era ... those were mostly gone, not available to future generations. So, my writing ... and my intent ... changed. I now wanted to have a record of *what* we did, *how* we did it, and *why* we did what we did. I wanted the reader to know what is possible when people commit to something bigger than they are. I wanted readers to know of our dreams, our hopes, our aspirations. And, I wanted you to know of the love we felt ... for our music, and for each other.

So here it is ... as accurately and as honestly as I could make it. I close with my last message to the players ... the love of my life, the Northern Iowa Wind Symphony.

June 29, 2017, 10:33am

Greetings,

Below, I have attached links to video productions of our final concert. I think there are some wonderful moments in each piece. I hope that you will be as proud of our accomplishments as am I.

I send my very best wishes to each of you ... with my hope that you find all that is available in this life. I offer a bit of advice gleaned from a book I just found:

The heart cannot be taught in a classroom intellectually, to students mechanically taking notes ... Good, wise hearts are obtained through lifetimes of diligent effort to dig deeply within and heal lifetimes of scars ... You can't teach it or email it or tweet it. It has to be discovered within the depths of one's own heart when a person is finally ready to go looking for it, and not before.

The job of the wise person is to swallow the frustration and just go on setting an example of caring and digging and diligence in their own lives. What a wise person teaches is the smallest part of what they give. The totality of their life, of the way they go about it in the smallest details, is what gets transmitted.

Never forget that. The message is the person, perfected over lifetimes of effort that was set in motion by yet another wise person now hidden from the recipient by the dim mists of time. Life is much bigger than we think, cause and effect intertwined in a vast moral structure that keeps pushing us to do better, become better, even when we dwell in the most painful confused darkness.

~ David Brooks, *The Road to Character* ~

Do the best you can . . . always! Take care of each other.

It was a great and life-altering adventure . . . what a ride!

rj

Appendices

Performance Repertoire

From the period, fall of 1982, until the spring of 2017, we have
programs indicating 811 performances of 458 separate pieces.
From our pattern of public performances during these years, it
seems there are maybe 10–12 programs missing for review. This is,
possibly, due to an inadequate system of program archives in the
School of Music. Also absent for review are the programs (12 or so)
performed by guest conductors during my two sabbaticals in 1991
and 2001, and my Fulbright year in Hungary during the 2004–2005
season.

Samuel Adler	Germany/USA	b. 1928	*A Little Night and Day Music*	1977	Full
Samuel Adler	Germany/USA	b. 1928	*Concert Piece*	1946	Chamber
Samuel Adler	Germany/USA	b. 1928	*The Merry Makers*	1982	Full
William Alwyn	England	1905–1985	*Fanfare for a Joyful Occasion*	1964	Chamber
Leroy Anderson	USA	1908–1990	*Bugler's Holiday*	1954	Full/Solo
Leroy Anderson	USA	1908–1990	*Drumbeat Jamboree*	1960	Full/Solo
Leroy Anderson	USA	1908–1975	*Trumpeter's Lullaby*	1950	Full/Solo
Louis Applebaum	Germany	1918–2000	*Suite of Miniature Dances*	1973	Full
Malcolm Arnold	England	1921–2006	*Trevalyan Suite*	1968	Chamber
Alexander Arutiunian	Armenia	1920–2012	*Concerto for Trumpet*	1950	Full/Solo
Blas Amelio Atehortúa	Colombia	b. 1943	*Musica para Orquestra de Vientos y Percussión* (*)	1989	Full
Georges Auric	France	1899–1983	*Le Palais Royal*	1936	Full
Jan Bach	USA	b. 1937	*Praetorius Suite*	1971	Full
Henk Badings	Holland	1907–1987	*Armageddon*	1968	Full/Solo
Henk Badings	Holland	1907–1987	*Concerto for Flute and Wind Symphony Orchestra*	1963	Full/Solo
Robert Baksa	USA	b. 1938	*Septet for Brass and Winds*	1992	Chamber
Árpad Balázs	Hungary	b. 1937	*Fanfárverbunk* (†)	1985	Full

* manuscript; † American premiere; ‡ World premiere; § Midwest premiere; | urtext

Jean Balissat	Switzerland	1936–2007	*Incantation et Sacrifice* (*, †)	1989	Full
Jean Balissat	Switzerland	1936–2007	*Le Premier Jour* (†)	1993	Full
James Barnes	USA	b. 1949	*For Natalie, from Symphony No. 3*	1994	Full
James Barnes	USA	b. 1949	*Lonely Beach*	1993	Full w/Women's Chorus
Jeremy Beck	USA	b. 1960	*Janus* (*, ✣)	1994	Full
James Beckel Jr.	USA	b. 1948	*The American Dream*	1992	Full
James Beckel Jr.	USA	b. 1948	*The Glass Bead Game*	1997	Full/Solo
David Bedford	England	1937–2011	*Sun Paints Rainbows on the Vast Waves*	1984	Full
Ludwig van Beethoven	Germany	1770–1827	*Four Pieces for Wind Ensemble*	1810	Chamber
Ludwig van Beethoven	Germany	1770–1827	*Military March, WoO 24*	1816	Full
Ludwig van Beethoven	Germany	1770–1827	*Octet op. 103*	1792	Chamber
Ludwig van Beethoven	Germany	1770–1827	*Rondino in E-flat*	1792	Chamber
Ludwig van Beethoven	Germany	1770–1827	*Siegessinfonie* (*)	1813	Full
Paul Ben-Chaim	Israel	1897–1984	*Fanfare to Israel*	1951	Full
Robert Russell Bennett	USA	1894–1981	*Rose Variations*	1955	Full/Solo
Warren Benson	USA	1924–2005	*Remembrance*	1965	Full
Warren Benson	USA	1924–2005	*The Passing Bell*	1983	Full
Hector Berlioz	France	1803–1869	*Symphonie Funebre et Triomphale*	1840	Full/Solo
Hector Berlioz/E. Kiel	France	1803–1869	*Hungarian March from Damnation of Faust*	1864	Full
Leonard Bernstein/Grundman	USA	1918–1990	*Suite from Candide*	1956	Full
William Bolcom	USA	b. 1938	*Song*	2001	Full
Eugene Bozza	France	1905–1991	*Ouverture pour Une Cérémonie*	1963	Chamber
Frank Bridge	England	1879–1941	*Music for a London Pageant*	1911	Full (w/Men's Chorus)
Benjamin Britten	England	1913–1976	*Fanfare for St. Edmundsbury*	1959	Chamber
Benjamin Britten	England	1913–1976	*Russian Funeral*	1936	Chamber
Isaac Brockshus	USA	b. 1988	*reset* (✣)	2016	Full
Timothy Broege	USA	b. 1947	*Sinfonia III, Quodlibet a 25*	1972	Full
Timothy Broege	USA	b. 1947	*Sinfonia V*	1973	Full
Timothy Broege	USA	b. 1947	*Songs Without Words*	1974	Full/Solo
Bruce Broughton	USA	b. 1945	*Excursions*	1995	Full/Solo
Bruce Broughton	USA	b. 1945	*Turbulence*	2013	Full/Solo
Steven Bryant	USA	b. 1972	*Alchemy in Silent Spaces*	2000	Full
Steven Bryant	USA	b. 1972	*Dusk*	2004	Full
Steven Bryant	USA	b. 1972	*Idyll*	2013	Full
Lewis Buckley	USA	b. 1947	*Bright Colored Dances*	1995	Full
Daniel Bukvich	USA	b. 1954	*Agincourt Hymn*	1987	Full
Daniel Bukvich	USA	b. 1954	*Hymn of St. Francis*	1992	Full
Daniel Bukvich	USA	b. 1954	*In Memoriam Dresden*	1978	Full
Daniel Bukvich	USA	b. 1954	*Maine Vigils* (*)	1990	Full
Daniel Bukvich	USA	b. 1954	*Meditations on the Writings of Vasily Kandinsky* (✣)	1996	Full/Solo
Daniel Bukvich	USA	b. 1954	*Surprise, Pattern, Illusion*	1985	Full/Solo
Daniel Bukvich	USA	b. 1954	*Symphonic Movement* (§)	2015-2016	Full
Daniel Bukvich	USA	b. 1954	*The Dream of Abraham* (✣)	1992	Full
Daniel Bukvich	USA	b. 1954	*Threnos*	1996	Full
Daniel Bukvich	USA	b. 1954	*Time Travel* (†)	1995	Full
Daniel Bukvich	USA	b. 1954	*Unusual Behavior in Ceremonies Involving Drums*	1999	Full/Solo
Daniel Bukvich	USA	b. 1954	*Voodoo*	1986	Full

* manuscript; † American premiere; ✣ World premiere; § Midwest premiere; | urtext

Mark Camphouse	USA	b. 1954	*Tribute*	1985	Full
Bruce Carlson	Canada	b. 1944	*Toledo*	1962	Full
John Barnes Chance	USA	1932–1974	*Incantation and Dance*	1963	Full
Bastiano Chilese	Italy	Late 16th c.	*Canzon Trigesimaquarta*	1608	Chamber
John Coda	USA	c. 1970	*Sinfonia Antiqua*	1987	Full
Shimon Cohen	Israel	b. 1937	*Fantasia on a Yemenite Traditional Song*	1992	Full
Michael Colgrass	Canada	b. 1932	*Bali*	2005	Full
William Connor	England	b. 1949	*Tails Aus Dem Vood Viennoise*	1992	Full
Aaron Copland	USA	1900–1990	*An Outdoor Overture*	1948	Full
Aaron Copland	USA	1900–1990	*Old American Songs*	1950-56	Full/Solo
Aaron Copland	USA	1900–1990	*Suite from The Red Pony*	1951-1969	Full
Aaron Copland	USA	1900–1990	*Variations on a Shaker Melody from Appalachian Spring*	1960	Full
Paul Creston	USA	1906–1985	*Legend*	1942	Full
James Curnow	USA	b. 1943	*Concertino for Tuba and Band*	1978	WS/Solo
Charles Cushing	USA	1905–1982	*Angel Camp* (*)	1952	Full
Ingolf Dahl	Germany/USA	1912–1970	*Concerto for Alto Saxophone and Wind Orchestra*	1949–53	Full/Solo
Ingolf Dahl	Germany/USA	1912–1970	*Sinfonietta*	1951	Full
Girolamo Dalla Casa	Italy	Late 16th c.	*Alix Avoit*	1584	Chamber/Solo
Nathan Daughtrey	USA	b. 1975	*Concerto for Vibraphone*	2012	Full/Solo
Nathan Daughtrey	USA	b. 1975	*Limerick Daydreams*	2006	Full
Jacob de Hahn	Holland	b. 1959	*Nerval's Poems*	2007	Full/Solo
Lorenzo Della Fonte	Italy	b. 1960	*Voci da Brescia, 1974*	1999	Full
Davide Delle Cese	Italy	1856–1938	*L'Inglesina*	1897	Full
Norman Dello Joio	USA	1913–2008	*Scenes from The Louvre*	1966	Full
Gaetano Donizetti	Italy	1797–1848	*Sinfonia in G minor*	1817	Chamber
Thomas Doss	Austria	b. 1966	*St. Florian Choral, In Memoriam Anton Bruckner*	2009	Full
Georg Druschetzky/Johnson	Bohemia	1745–1819	*Partita for Six Timpani*	1799	Full
Théodore Dubois	France	1837–1924	*Deuxieme Suite pour Instruments a Vent*	1898	Chamber
Pierre Max Dubois	France	1930–1995	*Quatour*	1958	Chamber
László Dubrovay	Hungary	b. 1943	*Das Lösengeld*	1999	Full
Thomas Duffy	USA	b. 1955	*A Song of Hiawatha*	1987	Full
Thomas Duffy	USA	b. 1955	*Crystals*	1985	Full
Thomas Duffy	USA	b. 1955	*Gnomon*	1998	Full
Antonín Dvořák	Bohemia	1841–1904	*Serenade op. 44*	1878	Chamber
Antonín Dvořák/Sheen	Bohemia	1841–1904	*Czech Suite, op. 39*	1879	Chamber
Martin Ellerby	England	b. 1957	*Paris Sketches*	1994	Full
Ferenc Erkel	Hungary	1810–1893	*Üennpi Zene (Festal Musik)* (*)	1860	Full
Ferenc Erkel	Hungary	1810–1893	*Ungarische Himnusz*	c. 1875	Full
Victor Ewald	Russia	1860–1935	*Symphony for Brass Choir*	c. 1912	Chamber
Ferrer Ferran	Spain	b. 1966	*Don Victor*	2003	Full
Henry Fillmore	USA	1881–1956	*His Honor*	1933	Full
Timo Forsström	Finland	b. 1961	*Sons of the Midnight Sun*	2012	Full (w/Men's Chorus)
Jean Francaix	France	1912–1997	*Le Gay Paris*	1974	Chamber/Solo
Jean Francaix	France	1912–1997	*Petite Fantasie pour contrebasse et instruments á vent sur la serenade "Don Giovanni"*	1981	Chamber/Solo
Jean Francaix	France	1912–1997	*Sept Dances*	1971	Chamber

* manuscript; † American premiere; ‡ World premiere; § Midwest premiere; | urtext

Mike Francis	USA	c. 1945	*Dreams of a Psychopath*	1969-71	Full/Solo
John Frantzen	USA	b. 1964	*Poem*	1998	Full
Girolamo Frescobaldi	Italy	1583–1643	*Capriccio Sopra La Battaglia*	1637	Chamber
Don Freund	USA	b. 1947	*Jug Blues and Fat Pickin'*	1986-90	Full
Julius Fucik	Bohemia	1872–1916	*Florentiner*	1898	Full
Gemba Fujita	Japan	1937–2013	*Lamentation of the Archangel Michael*	1978	Full
Giovanni Gabrieli	Italy	1553–1612	*Canzon Duodecimi Toni*	1612	Chamber
Giovanni Gabrieli	Italy	1553–1612	*Canzon per Sonare Quarti Toni*	1615	Chamber
Giovanni Gabrieli	Italy	1553–1612	*Canzon per Sonare Quarti Toni*	1597	Chamber
Giovanni Gabrieli	Italy	1554–1612	*Jubilate Deo*	1612	Chamber (w/ chorus)
Hans Gál	Austria	1890–1987	*Promenadenmusik für Militär-orchester*	1926	Full
Giorgio Gaslini	Italy	1929–2014	*Fellini's Song*	2000	Full
Ann Gebuhr	USA	b. 1945	*Trilogy*	1986	Chamber
George Gershwin/Skirrow	USA	1898–1937	*Scenes from Porgy and Bess*	1935-1996	Chamber
John Gibson	USA	b. 1946	*Resting in the Peace of His Hands*	1995	Full
David Gillingham	USA	b. 1947	*A Crescent Still Abides*	1998	Full
David Gillingham	USA	b. 1947	*Concertino for Four Percussion and Wind Orchestra*	1997	Full/Solo
David Gillingham	USA	b.1947	*No Shadow of Turning*	2005	Full
David Gillingham	USA	b. 1947	*With Heart and Voice*	2000	Full
Bernard Gilmore	USA	1937–2013	*Five Folk Songs for Soprano and Wind Orchestra*	1965	Full/Solo
Julie Giroux	USA	b. 1961	*Culloden*	2000	Full
Edwin Franko Goldman	USA	1878–1956	*On the Mall*	1923	Full
John Golland	England	1942–1993	*Atmospheres, op. 79*	1989	Full
Adam Gorb	England	b. 1958	*Suite for Winds*	1993	Chamber
Morton Gould	USA	1913–1996	*Suite from "Holocaust"*	1978	Full
Charles Gounod	France	1818–1893	*La Veau d' Or from Faust*	1859	Full/Solo
Charles Gounod	France	1818–1893	*Petite Symphonie*	1885	Chamber
Louis Théodore Gouvy	France	1819–1898	*Octet op. 71*	1879	Chamber
Louis Théodore Gouvy	France	1819–1898	*Petite Suite Gauloise*	1888	Chamber
Percy Aldridge Grainger	Australia/USA	1882–1961	*Blithe Bells* (*)	1931	Full
Percy Aldridge Grainger	Australia/USA	1882–1961	*Children's March, Over the Hills and Far Away*	1918	Full
Percy Aldridge Grainger	Australia/USA	1882–1961	*Colonial Song*	1918	Full
Percy Aldridge Grainger	Australia/USA	1882–1961	*Country Gardens*	1908-1936	Full
Percy Aldridge Grainger	Australia/USA	1882–1961	*Danish Folk Songs*	1926-41	Full
Percy Aldridge Grainger	Australia/USA	1882–1961	*Faeroe Island Dance*	c. 1926	Full
Percy Aldridge Grainger	Australia/USA	1882–1961	*Harvest Hymn*	1905-1940	Full
Percy Aldridge Grainger	Australia/USA	1882–1961	*Irish Tune from County Derry*	1918	Full
Percy Aldridge Grainger	Australia/USA	1882–1961	*Lincolnshire Posy*	1937	Full
Percy Aldridge Grainger	Australia/USA	1882–1961	*Marching Song of Democracy*	1900/1948 (ms)	Full
Percy Aldridge Grainger	Australia/USA	1882–1961	*Molly on the Shore*	1920	Full
Percy Aldridge Grainger	Australia/USA	1882–1961	*Sheep Shearing Song* (*)	1942	Full
Percy Aldridge Grainger	Australia/USA	1882–1961	*Shepherd's Hey*	1908-1918	Full
Percy Aldridge Grainger	Australia/USA	1882–1961	*Sussex Mummer's Christmas Carol*	1911	Full
Percy Aldridge Grainger	Australia/USA	1882–1961	*The Gumsuckers*	1942	Full
Percy Aldridge Grainger	Australia/USA	1882–1961	*The Lads of Wamphray*	1904	Full
Percy Aldridge Grainger	Australia/USA	1882–1961	*The Lonely Desert-Man Sees the Tents of the Happy Tribes* (*)	1950	Chamber
Percy Aldridge Grainger	Australia/USA	1882–1961	*The Merry King* (*)	1939	Chamber

* manuscript; † American premiere; ‡ World premiere; § Midwest premiere; | urtext

Percy Aldridge Grainger	Australia/USA	1882–1961	Tuscan Serenade (Faure) (*)	1937	Full
Percy Aldridge Grainger	Australia/USA	1882–1961	Walking Tune	1905-1940	Full
Percy Aldridge Grainger	Australia/USA	1882–1961	Ye Banks and Braes O' Bonnie Doon	1949	Full
Edward Gregson	England	b. 1945	Concerto for Tuba	1986	Full/Solo
Alexandre Guilmant	France	1837–1911	Morceau Symphonique	1902	Full/Solo
Frank Gulino	USA	b. 1987	Capriccio for Solo Trombone and Wind Ensemble	2010	Full/Solo
László Gulyás	Hungary	1928–1995	Széki Muzsika (Music from Szek)	1951	Full
Jozsef Gungl	Hungary	1810–1889	Magyar Indulo, op. 1	1836	Full
Reynaldo Hahn	Venezuela/France	1874–1947	Le Bal de Beatrice d' Este	1909	Chamber
Adolphus Hailstork	USA	b. 1941	American Guernica (*)	1982	Full
Adolphus Hailstork	USA	b. 1941	Out of the Depths (*)	1974	Full
Benjamin Hamehouts	Belgium	b. 1972	11th of September	2002	Full
Benjamin Hamehouts	Belgium	b. 1972	Honorisia	2002	Full
Peter Hamlin	USA	b. 1951	The City in the Sea	1987	Full
Peter Hamlin	USA	b. 1951	The Twelve Moons of Li He	1987	Chamber
Howard Hanson	USA	1896–1981	Dies Natalis	1972	Full
Howard Hanson	USA	1896–1981	Laude	1975	Full
Shelley Hanson	USA	b. 1951	Islas y Montanas	2003	Full
Johannes Hanssen	Norway	1874–1967	Valdres	1904	Full
Ronan Hardiman/Graham	England	b. 1961	Cry of the Celts	1996	Full
Walter S. Hartley	USA	1927–2016	Sinfonia No. 4	1965	Full
Franz Joseph Haydn	Austria	1732–1809	Divertimento No. 1, St. Antoni Chorale	1784	Chamber
Franz Joseph Haydn	Austria	1732–1809	Notturno in C, Hob. II: 32	1788–90	Chamber
Franz Joseph Haydn	Austria	1732–1809	Seven Last Words of Christ, Introduction, Part II	1799	Chamber
Franz Joseph Haydn	Austria	1732–1809	Three English Military Marches	1792-1794	Chamber
Samuel Hazo	USA	b. 1966	Blessings	2005	Full/Solo
Samuel Hazo	USA	b. 1966	Each Time You Tell Their Story	2003	Full
Samuel Hazo	USA	b. 1966	Fantasy on a Japanese Folk Song	2005	Full
Samuel Hazo	USA	b. 1966	In Flight	2000	Full
Samuel Hazo	USA	b. 1966	In Heaven's Air	2001	Full
Samuel Hazo	USA	b. 1966	Their Blossoms Down	2001	Full
J. C. Heed	USA	1862–1908	In Storm and Sunshine	1905	Full
Hans Werner Henze	Germany	1926–2012	Die Abenteuer des Don Quixote	1990	Full
Hans Werner Henze	Germany	1926–2012	Ragtimes and Habaneras	1975	Full
Frigyes Hidas	Hungary	1928–2007	Almost B.A.C.H. (*, ⚹)	1993	Full
Frigyes Hidas	Hungary	1928–2007	Capriccio	1996	Full
Frigyes Hidas	Hungary	1928–2007	Circus Suite (†)	1985	Full
Frigyes Hidas	Hungary	1928–2007	Concertino for Tuba and Band	1981	Full
Frigyes Hidas	Hungary	1928–2007	Concertino for Wind Orchestra	1981	Full
Frigyes Hidas	Hungary	1928–2007	Concerto for Bassoon	1999	Chamber
Frigyes Hidas	Hungary	1928–2007	Concerto for Saxophone Quartet and Wind Orchestra	1998	Full/Solo
Frigyes Hidas	Hungary	1928–2007	Concerto for Tuba and Wind Orchestra	1996	Full/Solo
Frigyes Hidas	Hungary	1928–2007	Concerto No. 2 for Oboe and Wind Ensemble	2000	Chamber/Solo
Frigyes Hidas	Hungary	1928–2007	Double Concerto (oboe & bassoon)	2001	Chamber/Solo
Frigyes Hidas	Hungary	1928–2007	Fantasy for Violoncello and Wind Orchestra (⚹)	1998	Chamber/Solo
Frigyes Hidas	Hungary	1928–2007	Music for Brass Instruments	1985	Chamber

* manuscript; † American premiere; ⚹ World premiere; $ Midwest premiere; | urtext

Frigyes Hidas	Hungary	1928–2007	*Music for the Fourth European Music Festival*	1995	Full w/children's chorus
Frigyes Hidas	Hungary	1928–2007	*Pictures of South Africa*	2007	Full
Frigyes Hidas	Hungary	1928–2007	*Quintetto Concertante for Brass Quintet and Wind Orchestra* (†)	1992	Full/Solo
Frigyes Hidas	Hungary	1928–2007	*Remembrance*	1996	Full
Frigyes Hidas	Hungary	1928–2007	*Requiem* (†)	1996	Full w/Chorus & Solists
Frigyes Hidas	Hungary	1928–2007	*Symphonic Movement*	2002	Full
Frigyes Hidas	Hungary	1928–2007	*Vidám Zene (Merry Music)*	1983	Full
William Himes	USA	b. 1949	*Amazing Grace*		Full
Paul Hindemith	Germany	1895–1963	*Hin und Zuruck*, op. 45a	1927	Chamber Opera
Paul Hindemith	Germany	1895–1963	*Symphony in B-flat*	1951	Full
Paul Hindemith/Wilson	Germany	1895–1963	*March from Symphonic Metamorphosis*	1943	Full
Hans Hindpere	Estonia	1928–2012	*Jaunatnes Svetki*		Full
Lajos Hollós	Hungary	b. 1954	*Körispataki Czárdás*	1978	Full
Gustav Holst	England	1874–1934	*Hammersmith*	1930	Full
Gustav Holst	England	1874–1934	*Moorside Suite*	1928	Full
Gustav Holst	England	1874–1934	*Music for a London Pageant* (*)	1911	Full (w/Men's Chorus
Gustav Holst	England	1874–1934	*Suite in E-flat for Military Band* (|)	1909	Full
Gustav Holst	England	1874–1934	*Suite in F* (|)	1911	Full
Gustav Holst	England	1874–1934	*Three Folk Tunes* (*)	1921	Full
Arthur Honegger	France	1892–1955	*Marche sur la Bastille*	1936	Full
Joseph Horovitz	England	b. 1926	*Bacchus on Blue Ridge*	1983	Full
Alan Hovhaness	Armenia/USA	1911–2000	*Prayer of St. Gregory*, op. 62b	1952	Full/Solo
Alan Hovhaness	Armenia/USA	1911–2000	*Symphony No. 4*	1958	Full
Jenö Hubáy/Marosi	Hungary	1858–1937	*Hejre, Kati!*	1884	Full
Heinrich Hubler	Germany	1822–1893	*Concerto for Four Horns*	1854	Full
Ralph Hultgren	Australia	b. 1953	*Bright Sunlit Morning*	2001	Full/Solo
Ralph Hultgren	Australia	b. 1953	*My Sister's Tears*	2006	Full
Ralph Hultgren	Australia	b. 1953	*Symphony for Wind Orchestra* (*, ‡)	1994	Full
Ralph Hultgren	Australia	b. 1953	*The Hornet's Nest*	1988	Full
Karel Husa	Czech/USA	1921–2016	*Apotheosis of This Earth*	1970	Full
Karel Husa	Czech/USA	1921–2016	*Concerto for Percussion and Wind Ensemble*	1972	Full/Solo
Karel Husa	Czech/USA	1921–2016	*Divertimento for Brass and Percussion*	1959	Chamber
Karel Husa	Czech/USA	1921–2016	*Music for Prague, 1968*	1968	Full
Karel Husa	Czech/USA	1921–2016	*Smetana Fanfare*	1984	Full
Jenö Huszka	Hungary	1875–1960	*Bob Herceg, Nyitány*	1902	Full
Anthony Iannaccone	USA	b. 1943	*After a Gentle Rain*	1981	Full
Jacques Ibert	France	1890–1962	*14 Juillet Overture*	1936	Full
Jacques Ibert	France	1890–1962	*Concerto pour Violoncelle et Orchestre d' Instruments a Vent*	1926	Chamber/Solo
Yasuhide Ito	Japan	b. 1960	*Glorioso*	1990	Full
Charles Ives/Elkus	USA	1874–1954	*Old Home Days*	c. 1900	Full
Charles Ives/Elkus	USA	1874–1954	*The Alcotts*	1947	Full
Gordon Jacob	England	1895–1984	*Fantasia*	1973	Full/Solo
Gordon Jacob	England	1895–1984	*Old Wine in New Bottles*	1960	Chamber
Gordon Jacob	England	1895–1984	*William Byrd Suite*	1924	Full
Robert Jager	USA	b. 1939	*Esprit de Corps*	1985	Full
Zdenek Jonák	Czech	1917–1995	*Ciacona in E Minor* (*)	1993	Full

* manuscript; † American premiere; ‡ World premiere; $ Midwest premiere; \| urtext

Daniel Kallman	USA	b. 1956	*A Halama Christmas*	2004	Chamber
Daniel Kallman	USA	b. 1956	*An American Tapestry*	2004	Chamber
Herbert von Karajan (arr.)	Germany	1908–1989	*The European Anthem*	1972	Full
Juris Karlsons	Latvia	b. 1948	*Svetku Uvertira*	c.2002	Full
Aram Khatchaturian	Armenia	1903–1978	*Armenian Folk Songs*	1932	Full
Aram Khatchaturian	Armenia	1903–1978	*Soviet Police March*	1973	Full
Thomas Knox	USA	1937–2004	*God of Our Fathers*	1988	Full
Thomas Knox	USA	1937–2004	*Sea Songs*	1980	Full
Charles Knox	USA	b. 1929	*Voluntary on Lauda Anima*	1983	Chamber
Zoltán Kodály	Hungary	1882–1967	*Hary Janos Suite*	1926	Chamber
János Nepomuk Král	Bohemia	1839–1896	*Hoch Habsburg!*	1882	Full
Stéphane Kreger	France		*Concerto for Clarinet*	2012	Full/Solo
Ernst Krenek	Austria/USA	1900–1991	*Drei Lustige Marsche, op. 44*	1926	Chamber
Frantisek Krommer	Bohemia	1759–1831	*Concerto á Due Corni*	1799	Chamber/Solo
Robert Kurka	USA	1921–1957	*The Good Soldier Schweik Suite, op. 22*	1956	Chamber
Pierre Leemans	Belgium	1897–1980	*Marche des Parachutistes Belges*	1944	Full
Ferenc Lehár Jr.	Slovakia	1870–1948	*Gypsy Love*	1910	Full
Ferenc Lehár Jr.	Slovakia	1870–1948	*It Starts Just Now*	c. 1893	Full
Ferenc Lehár Jr./Reed	Slovakia	1870–1948	*Vilja aus Die Lustige Witwe*	1905	Full
Ferenc Lehár Sr.	Hungary	1838–1898	*Oliosi Sturm Marsch*	1866	Full
Kamilló Lendvay	Hungary	1928–2016	*Concertino for Piano, Winds, Percussion and Harp*	1960–1982	Full/Solo
Kamilló Lendvay	Hungary	1928–2016	*Concerto for Trumpet* (†)	1990	Full/Solo
Kamilló Lendvay	Hungary	1928–2016	*Festspiel Overture*	1984	Full
Kamilló Lendvay	Hungary	1928–2016	*Hárόm Farsangi Maszk (Three Carnival Masks)*	1960	Full
Ferenc Liszt/Hidas	Hungary	1811–1886	*Rákóczi Induló*	1865	Full
Zdenek Lukás	Czech	1928–2007	*Musica Boema*	1976	Full
Zdenek Lukás	Czech	1928–2007	*Prager Festmusik*	1999	Full
Edward MacDowell	USA	1862–1908	*Woodland Sketches*	1896-1923	Full
John Mackey	USA	b. 1973	*Sheltering Sky*	2012	Full
Roy Magnuson	USA	b. 1985	*Harvest Moon*	2006	Full
Gustav Mahler	Austria	1860–1911	*Um Mitternacht*	1904	Chamber/Solo
Timothy Mahr	USA	b. 1956	*Fantasia in G, Freude, Schöner Götterfunken*	1983	Full
David Maslanka	USA	1953–2017	*Give Us This Day, Short Symphony for Wind Ensemble*	2007	Full
David Maslanka	USA	1943–2017	*Mother Earth*	2005	Full
David Maslanka	USA	1943–2017	*Requiem*	2013	Full
Tiburtio Massaino	Italy	1557–1615	*Canzon Trigesimaquinta*	1608	Chamber
Rudolf Mayer	Czech	1902–1983	*Festmusik für acht Horner*	1979	Full/Solo
Scott McAllister	USA	b. 1969	*Black Dog*	2003	Full/Solo
Francis McBeth	USA	1933–2012	*Beowulf*	1986	Full
Francis McBeth	USA	1933–2012	*Kaddish*	1976	Full
Francis McBeth	USA	1933–2012	*When Honor Whispers and Shouts*	1998	Full
Mark McCoy	USA	b. 1964	*A Symphony for Salem, 1692*	1994	Full
Felix Mendelssohn/Johnson	Germany	1809–1847	*Overture für Harmoniemusik*	1824	Full
Hardy Mertens	Holland	b.1960	*Se Oghe é Su Bentu, op. 207*	1997	Full
Hardy Mertens	Holland	b. 1960	*The Butterfly Lovers*	2008	Full/Solo
Hardy Mertens	Holland	b. 1960	*Xenia Sarda*	1996	Full
Darius Milhaud	France	1892–1974	*La Création du Monde*	1923	Chamber
Darius Milhaud	France	1892–1974	*Suite Francaise*	1944	Full

* manuscript; † American premiere; ‡ World premiere; § Midwest premiere; | urtext

Wolfgang Amadeus Mozart	Austria	1756–1791	Divertimento in B-flat, K. 186	1773	Chamber
Wolfgang Amadeus Mozart	Austria	1756–1791	Divertimento in E-flat, K. 166	1773	Chamber
Wolfgang Amadeus Mozart	Austria	1756–1791	Gran Partita, K. 370a	1781	Chamber
Wolfgang Amadeus Mozart	Austria	1756–1791	Österreichische Bundeshymne		Full
Wolfgang Amadeus Mozart	Austria	1756–1791	Partita II		Chamber
Wolfgang Amadeus Mozart	Austria	1756–1791	Partita in C Minor, K. 384A	1784	Chamber
Wolfgang Amadeus Mozart	Austria	1756–1791	Partita in E-flat, K.375	1781	Chamber
Wolfgang Amadeus Mozart	Austria	1756–1791	Partita IV in B-flat	1784-1792	Chamber
Robert Muczynski	USA	1929–2010	Movements	1967	Chamber
Modest Mussorgsky	Russia	1839–1881	Mephistopheles' Song in Auerbach's Cellar	1879	Full/Solo
Modest Mussorgsky	Russia	1839–1881	Song of the Flea	1879	Full/Solo
Vaclav Nelhybel	Czech/USA	1919–1996	Symphonic Movement	1966	Full
Vaclav Nelhybel	Czech	1919–1996	Trittico	1963	Full
Ron Nelson	USA	b. 1929	Fanfare for the Hour of Sunrise (*)	1989	Full
Ron Nelson	USA	b. 1929	Medieval Suite	1982	Full
Ron Nelson	USA	b. 1929	Morning Alleluias (*)	1990	Full
Ron Nelson	USA	b. 1929	Resonances I	1990	Full
Jonathan Newman	USA	b. 1972	As the Scent of Spring Rain . . .	2003	Full
Jonathan Newman	USA	b. 1972	Moon by Night	2004	Full
Harold Noble	England	1903–1998	Hertfordshire Suite	1984	Chamber
Sandy Nordahl	USA	b. 1964	Pinecones and Penrose Tiles (‡)	2002	Full/Solo
Rudolf Nováček	Bohemia	1860–1929	Sinfonietta, op. 48	1888	Chamber
Carl Orff/ J. Krance	Germany	1895–1982	Carmina Burana	1936	Full
Carl Orff/F. Wanken	Germany/USA	1895–1982	Carmina Burana	1936	Chamber
Joseph Ott	USA	1929–1990	Africotta II (*)	1979	Full
Annibale Padovano	Italy	1527–1575	Aria Della Battaglia	1568	Chamber
John Paulson	USA	b. 1948	Epinicion	1975	Full
Jozsef Pécsi	Hungary	1874–1958	Unter Der Siegesflagge	c. 1914	Full
John Pennington	USA	b. 1939	Apollo	1971	Full
Ernst Pepping	Germany	1901–1981	Kleine Serenade für Blasorchester	1926	Chamber
Vincent Persichetti	USA	1915–1987	Divertimento for Band, op. 42	1950	Full
Boris Pigovat	Russia/Israel	b. 1953	Masada (†)	1997	Full
Boris Pigovat	Israel	b. 1953	Shalom Aleykhem	2000	Full
Carlo Pirola	Italy	b. 1945	I Temi della Memoria	1999	Full
Walter Piston	USA	1894–1976	Tunbridge Fair	1950	Full
Carlo Alberto Pizzini	Italy	1905–1981	Al Piemonte	1941	Full
Anthony Plog	USA	b. 1947	Animal Ditties IV	1991	Chamber
Anthony Plog	USA	b. 1947	Mini-Variations on Amazing Grace	1993	Chamber
Amilcare Ponchielli	Italy	1834–1886	Elegie Sulla Tomba di Garibaldi	1882	Full
Amilcare Ponchielli	Italy	1834–1886	Gran Marcia Trionfale, "Milano"	1899	Full
Niccola Porpora	Italy	1686–1768	Overture Roiala	1768	Chamber
Michael Praetorius	Germany	1571–1621	Dance Suite from "Terpsichore"	1612	Full
Serge Prokofiev	Russia	1891–1953	March, op. 99	1943	Full
Serge Prokofiev/D. Law	Russia	1891–1953	Lieutenant Kiji Fantasy	1933/1985 (ms)	Full
Giacomo Puccini	Italy	1858–1924	Nessun Dorma from Turandot	1924	Full/Solo
Serge Rachmaninov	Russia	1873–1943	Aleko's Cavatina from Aleko	1892	Full/Solo
György Ranki	Hungary	1907–1993	Suite from Pomádé Király Uj Ruhája	1954	Full
György Ranki	Hungary	1907–1993	Suite from The Magic Potion (†)	1974	Full
Maurice Ravel/Grainger	France	1875–1937	La Vallee des Cloches (*)	1944ʻ	Chamber
Alfred Reed	USA	1921–2005	Ballade for Alto Saxophone and Band	1956	Full/Solo
Alfred Reed	USA	1921–2005	Othello	1977	Full

* manuscript; † American premiere; ‡ World premiere; $ Midwest premiere; | urtext

Ottorino Respighi	Italy	1879–1936	*Huntingtower*	1932	Full
Marga Richter	USA	b. 1926	*Country Auction*	1976	Full
Nikolai Rimsky-Korsakov	Russia	1844–1908	*Concerto for Trombone and Military Band*	1877	Full/Solo
Nikolai Rimsky-Korsakov	Russia	1844–1908	*Cortege aus Mlada*	1892	Full
Nikolai Rimsky-Korsakov	Russia	1844–1908	*Konzertstück in Eb for Clarinet and Military Band*	1878	Full/Solo
Nikolai Rimsky-Korsakov	Russia	1844–1908	*Variations on a Theme of Glinka*	1878	Full/Solo
Joaquin Rodrigo	Spain	1901–1999	*Adagio para Orquestra de Instrumentos de Viente*	1966	Full
Bernard Rogers	USA	1893–1968	*Tribal Drums from Africa Symphony*	1966	Full
Philip Rothman	USA	b. 1976	*Monument Fanfare and Tribute*	2000	Full
Rolf Rudin	Germany	b. 1961	*Amen*	2013	Full
Rolf Rudin	Germany	b. 1961	*Requiem, op. 70*	2005	Full w/Chorus & Solists
Rolf Rudin	Germany	b. 1961	*Te Deum, op. 93* (✲)	2016-2017	Full (w/Men's Chorus)
Rolf Rudin	Germany	b. 1961	*The Pale Moon*	1997	Full
Robert Rumbelow	USA	b. 1965	*Amazing Grace*	2003	Full
Robert Rumbelow	USA	b. 1965	*Night*	2002	Full
Ernst Sachse	Germany	1813–1870	*Concertino in E-flat*	1845	Full/Solo
Camille Saint-Saëns	France	1835–1921	*Grande Marche, Occident et Orient*	1869	Full
Antonio Salieri	Italy	1750–1825	*Armonia per un Tempio della Notte* (*)	c. 1785	Chamber
Arnold Schönberg	Austria	1874–1951	*Theme and Variations, op. 43A*	1943	Full
Franz Schubert	Austria	1797–1828	*Deutsche Mess in F, D 872*	1827	Chamber (w/ chorus)
Gunther Schuller (arr.)	USA	1925–2015	*Tribute to Rudy Wiedoeft*	1917-1923	Chamber/Solo
William Schuman	USA	1910–1992	*New England Triptych*	1957	Full
Robert Schumann	Germany	1810–1856	*Beim Abschied zu Singen, op. 84*	1848	Chamber (w/ chorus)
Joseph Schwantner	USA	b. 1943	*From a Dark Millennium*	1981	Full
James Sclater	USA	b. 1943	*Soundings*	1982	Chamber
Dmitri Shostakovich	Russia	1906–1975	*March of the Soviet Police*	1970	Full
Dmitri Shostakovich	Russia	1906–1975	*Suite for Variety Orchestra*	c. 1956	Full
Jean Sibelius	Norway	1865–1957	*Tiera*	c. 1891	Full
Gardell Simons	USA	1878–1945	*Atlantic Zephyrs*	1915	Full/Solo
John Stafford Smith/Zaninelli	USA		*Star Spangled Banner*		Full
Kenneth Snoeck	USA	b. 1946	*Symphony No. 3, "Scaramouch"*		
Jerome Sorcsek	USA	b. 1951	*Portrait of Faustus* (*)	1978	Full
John Philip Sousa	USA	1854–1932	*Nobles of the Mystic Shrine*	1923	Full
John Philip Sousa	USA	1854–1932	*Semper Fidelis*	1888	Full
John Philip Sousa	USA	1854–1932	*Songs of Grace and Songs of Glory*	1893	Full
John Philip Sousa	USA	1854–1932	*The Black Horse Troop*	1924	Full
Philip Sparke	England	b. 1951	*Mandalen Landscapes*	2004	Full
Louis Spohr	Germany	1784–1859	*Notturno for Turkish Band, op. 34*	1815	Chamber
Pavel Stanek	Czech	b. 1927	*Bohemian Folk Dance Suite*	1998	Full
Noel Stockton	South Africa	b. 1930	*Manguang* (*)	1988	Full
Richard Strauss	Germany	1864–1959	*Serenade op. 7*	1882	Chamber
Tielman Susato/Dunnigan	Holland	1510–1570	*Suite from La Danserye*	1551	Full
Tielman Susato/Johnson	Holland	1510–1570	*Suite for Brass*	1551	Chamber
Tielman Susato/Johnson	Holland	1510–1570	*Suite from Dansyere*	1557	Full
Jan Sweelinck/Ricker	Holland	1562–1621	*Variations on "Mein Junges Leben hat ein End"*	1975	Full
James Syler	USA	b. 1961	*Fields*	1994	Full
James Syler	USA	b. 1961	*Tattoo*	2005	Full

* manuscript; † American premiere; ✲ World premiere; $ Midwest premiere; | urtext

Masuro Tanaka	Japan	b. 1946	*Methuselah II*	1988	Full
Alexander Tcherepnin	Russia	1899–1977	*Fanfare*	1964	Chamber
Carl Teike	Germany	1864–1922	*Alte Kameraden*	1889	Full
Virgil Thomson	USA	1896–1989	*A Solemn Music*	1949	Full
Frank Ticheli	USA	b. 1958	*Angels in the Architecture*	2008	Full
Frank Ticheli	USA	b. 1958	*Sanctuary*	2005	Full
Frank Ticheli	USA	b. 1958	*Shenendoah*	1999	Full
Ernst Toch	Germany	1887–1864	*Spiel für Blasorchester, op. 39*	1926	Full
Josef Triebensee	Austria	1772–1846	*Partita Variations*	early 19th c.	Chamber
Fisher Tull	USA	1934–1994	*The Binding*	1981	Chamber
Bernard van Beurden	Holland	1933–2016	*Concerto for Bassoon, Winds and Percussion* (‡)	1992	Chamber
Bernard van Beurden	Holland	1933–2016	*Estampie*	1972-1992	Chamber
Ralph Vaughan Williams	England	1872–1958	*England's Pleasant Land* (*)	1938	Full (w/Men's Chorus)
Ralph Vaughan Williams	England	1872–1958	*English Folk Songs*	1923	Full
Ralph Vaughan Williams	England	1872–1958	*Scherzo alla Marcia, from Symphony No. 8 in D Minor*	1956	Chamber
Ralph Vaughan Williams	England	1872–1958	*Sea Songs*	1923	Full
Giuseppe Verdi	Italy	1813–1901	*Infelice! . . . e tuo credivi from Ernani*	1844	Full/Solo
Bozo Vojnovich	Croatia		*Triptychon* (*)	1968	Full
Richard Wagner	Germany	1813–1883	*Elisabeth's Prayer from Tannhäuser*	1845	Chamber/Solo
Richard Wagner	Germany	1813–1883	*Huldigungsmarsch*	1864	Full
Richard Wagner	Germany	1813–1883	*Introduction to Scene IV, Act II, Lohengrin*	1850	Full
Richard Wagner	Germany	1813–1883	*Trauermusik*	1844	Full
Richard Wagner/Bainum	Germany	1813–1883	*"Liebestod" from Tristan und Isolde*	1859	Full
Peter Warlock/Geddes	England	1894–1930	*Capriol Suite*	1926	Chamber
Robert Washut	USA	b. 1951	*The High Road* (‡)	2013	Full/Solo
Carl Maria von Weber	Germany	1786–1826	*Concertino for Oboe*		Chamber/Solo
Kurt Weill	Germany	1900–1950	*Kleine Dreigroschenmusik*	1928	Chamber
Dan Welcher	USA	b. 1948	*The Yellowstone Fires*	1988	Full
Floyd Werle	USA	b. 1929	*Golden Age of the Xylophone*	1999	Full/Solo
Eric Whitacre	USA	b. 1970	*October*	2000	Full
Eric Whitacre	USA	b. 1970	*Seal Lullaby*	2011	Full
Jillian Whitaker	USA	b. 1992	*Coming Home* (‡)	2016	Full
David Whitwell	USA	b. 1937	*Chorale Variations on "Vater unser in Himmelreich"* (‡)	2010	Full
David Whitwell	USA	b. 1937	*Civil War Reflections*	1995	Full/Solo
David Whitwell	USA	b. 1937	*Jubilaüm*	1997	Full
David Whitwell	USA	b. 1937	*Sinfonia da Requiem, in memory of Mozart*	1988	Full
David Whitwell	USA	b.1937	*Symphony No. 6, II. Faith*	2015	Full
Alec Wilder	USA	1907–1980	*A Debutante's Diary*	1939	Chamber
Alec Wilder	USA	1907–1980	*She'll be Seven in May*	1939	Chamber
Alec Wilder	USA	1907–1980	*Such a Tender Night*	1939	Chamber
Alec Wilder	USA	1907–1980	*Walking Home in Spring*	1942	Chamber
Clifton Williams	USA	1923–1976	*Fanfare and Allegro*	1956	Full
John Williams	USA	b. 1932	*1941*	1979	Full
John Williams	USA	b. 1932	*Hymn to the Fallen*	1998	Full
John Williams	USA	b. 1932	*Music from "Schindler's List"*	1993	Full/Solo
John Williams	USA	b. 1932	*Music from "Star Wars"*	1977	Full

* manuscript; † American premiere; ‡ World premiere; $ Midwest premiere; | urtext

John Williams	USA	b. 1932	*Raiders March from Raiders of the Lost Ark*	1981	Full
John Williams	USA	b. 1932	*Summon the Heroes*	1996	Full
Clifton Williams	USA	1923–1976	*Symphonic Dance No. 3, "Fiesta"*	1967	Full
Clifton Williams	USA	1923–1976	*Symphonic Suite*	1957	Full
Clifton Williams	USA	1923–1976	*The Sinfonians*	1960	Full
Dana Wilson	USA	b. 1946	*Shortcut Home*	2003	Full
Guy Woolfenden	England	b. 1937	*Gallimaufrey*	1982	Full
Guy Woolfenden	England	b. 1937	*Illyrian Dances*	1986	Full
Guy Woolfenden	England	b. 1937	*Serenade for Sophia*	2001	Chamber
Guy Woolfenden	England	b. 1937	*Suite Francaise*	1991	Chamber
Satoshi Yagisawa	Japan	b. 1975	*Hymn to the Sun–With the Beat of Mother Earth*	2005	Full
Bruce Yurko	USA	b. 1951	*Danza No. 2*	2003	Full
Benjamin Yusupov	Tajikistan/Israel	b. 1962	*Sounds of Fanfares*	1994	Full
Benjamin Yusupov	Tajikistan/Israel	b. 1962	*Suite for Wind Orchestra*	1993–94	Full
Luigi Zananelli	Italy/USA	b. 1932	*Lagan Love*	1999	Full
Luigi Zaninelli	Italy/USA	b. 1932	*The Magic Ballroom*	2003	Full

* manuscript; † American premiere; ‡ World premiere; $ Midwest premiere; | urtext

Core Repertoire

I have designated, as Core Repertoire, all works which were performed three or more times in separate concert seasons. I imple-
mented this designation in my doctoral thesis, "Wind Ensembles in
Six American Collegiate Institutions" (University of Illinois, 1986), a
designation used in several subsequent studies.

There are 59 compositions designated as Core Repertoire, works
for both full ensemble (Wind Symphony) and chamber ensemble
(Chamber Wind Players).

Robert Russell Bennett	USA	1894–1981	*Rose Variations*	1955	Full/Solo
Leonard Bernstein/Grundman	USA	1918–1990	*Suite from Candide*	1956	Full
Benjamin Britten	England	1913–1976	*Fanfare for St. Edmundsbury*	1959	Chamber
William Connor	England	b. 1949	*Tails Aus Dem Vood Viennoise*	1992	Full
Charles Cushing	USA	1905–1982	*Angel Camp* (*)	1952	Full
Julius Fucik	Bohemia	1872–1916	*Florentiner*	1898	Full
George Gershwin/Skirrow	USA	1898–1937	*Scenes from Porgy and Bess*	1935–1996	Chamber
David Gillingham	USA	b. 1947	*Concertino for Four Percussion and Wind Orchestra*	1997	Full/Solo
Julie Giroux	USA	b. 1961	*Culloden*	2000	Full
Morton Gould	USA	1913–1996	*Suite from "Holocaust"*	1978	Full
Charles Gounod	France	1818–1893	*Petite Symphonie*	1885	Chamber
Louis Théodore Gouvy	France	1819–1898	*Octet op. 71*	1879	Chamber
Percy Aldridge Grainger	Australia/USA	1882–1961	*Children's March, Over the Hills and Far Away*	1918	Full
Percy Aldridge Grainger	Australia/USA	1882–1961	*Colonial Song*	1918	Full
Percy Aldridge Grainger	Australia/USA	1882–1961	*Country Gardens*	1908–1936	Full
Percy Aldridge Grainger	Australia/USA	1882–1961	*Molly on the Shore*	1920	Full
Percy Aldridge Grainger	Australia/USA	1882–1961	*The Gumsuckers*	1942	Full
Percy Aldridge Grainger	Australia/USA	1882–1961	*Ye Banks and Braes O' Bonnie Doon*	1949	Full
Frigyes Hidas	Hungary	1928–2007	*Concertino for Wind Orchestra*	1981	Full
Frigyes Hidas	Hungary	1928–2007	*Vidám Zene (Merry Music)*	1983	Full
Paul Hindemith	Germany	1895–1963	*Symphony in B-flat*	1951	Full
Gustav Holst	England	1874–1934	*Music for a London Pageant* (*)	1911	Full (w/Men's Chorus)
Gustav Holst	England	1874–1934	*Suite in E-flat for Military Band* (|)	1909	Full
Gustav Holst	England	1874–1934	*Suite in F* (|)	1911	Full
Jenö Hubáy/Marosi	Hungary	1858–1937	*Hejre, Kati!*	1884	Full
Karel Husa	Czech/USA	1921–2016	*Apotheosis of This Earth*	1970	Full
Karel Husa	Czech/USA	1921–2016	*Smetana Fanfare*	1984	Full
Gordon Jacob	England	1895–1984	*Old Wine in New Bottles*	1960	Chamber
Ernst Krenek	Austria/USA	1900–1991	*Drei Lustige Marsche, op. 44*	1926	Chamber
Frantisek Krommer	Bohemia	1759–1831	*Concerto á Due Corni*	1799	Chamber/Solo
Pierre Leemans	Belgium	1897–1980	*Marche des Parachutistes Belges*	1944	Full
Gustav Mahler	Austria	1860–1911	*Um Mitternacht*	1904	Chamber/Solo
Scott McAllister	USA	b. 1969	*Black Dog*	2003	Full/Solo
Hardy Mertens	Holland	b. 1960	*Xenia Sarda*	1996	Full

* manuscript; † American premiere; ‡ World premiere; $ Midwest premiere; | urtext

Wolfgang Amadeus Mozart	Austria	1756–1791	*Partita in E-flat, K.375*	1781	Chamber
Ron Nelson	USA	b. 1929	*Medieval Suite*	1982	Full
Ron Nelson	USA	b. 1929	*Resonances I*	1990	Full
Harold Noble	England	1903–1998	*Hertfordshire Suite*	1984	Chamber
Rudolf Nováček	Bohemia	1860–1929	*Sinfonietta, op. 48*	1888	Chamber
Vincent Persichetti	USA	1915–1987	*Divertimento for Band, op. 42*	1950	Full
György Rankí	Hungary	1907–1993	*Suite from The Magic Potion* (†)	1989	Full
Alfred Reed	USA	1921–2005	*Othello*	1977	Full
Nikolai Rimsky-Korsakov	Russia	1844–1908	*Cortege aus Mlada*	1892	Full
Joaquin Rodrigo	Spain	1901–1999	*Adagio para Orquestra de Instrumentos de Viente*	1966	Full
Camille Saint-Saëns	France	1835–1921	*Grande Marche, Occident et Orient*	1869	Full
William Schuman	USA	1910–1992	*New England Triptych*	1957	Full
Dmitri Shostakovich	Russia	1906–1975	*Suite for Variety Orchestra*	c. 1956	Full
Jerome Sorcsek	USA	b. 1951	*Portrait of Faustus* (*)	1978	Full
Richard Strauss	Germany	1864–1959	*Serenade op. 7*	1882	Chamber
Ralph Vaughan Williams	England	1872–1958	*English Folk Songs*	1923	Full
Ralph Vaughan Williams	England	1872–1958	*The Pageant of London*	1911	Full (w/Men's Chorus)
Bozo Vojnovich	Croatia		*Triptychon*	1968	Full
Richard Wagner	Germany	1813–1883	*Huldigungsmarsch*	1864	Full
Richard Wagner	Germany	1813–1883	*Trauermusik*	1844	Full
Kurt Weill	Germany	1900–1950	*Kleine Dreigroschenmusik*	1928	Chamber
Eric Whitacre	USA	b. 1970	*October*	2000	Full
David Whitwell	USA	b. 1937	*Sinfonia da Requiem, in memory of Mozart*	1988	Full
Guy Woolfenden	England	b. 1937	*Illyrian Dances*	1986	Full
Guy Woolfenden	England	b. 1937	*Suite Francaise*	1991	Chamber

* manuscript; † American premiere; ‡ World premiere; $ Midwest premiere; | urtext

Wind Symphony, 1982–2017

Flute

Claudia Aizaga
Jennifer Baker
Eliza Bangert
Cheri Bass
Maureen Becker
Amy Bell
Katharine Benya
Emily Bicknese
Breta Borstad
Hannah Carr-Murphy
Linnea Casey
Dominique Cawley
Abigail Coffer
Sarah Cosgrove
Renee Crandall
Nicole Davis
Shaina Rush Davis
Deborah Dellinger
Andrea Dipofi
Shivhan Dose
Makenzie Doyle
Heather DuBrall
Heather Egts
Stacy Fahrion
Jennifer Fawcett
Melanie Ferjak
Erin Franklin
Crystal Franzen
Brielle Frost
Sarah Goodenow
Rylie Graham
Betsy Groat
Rocio Lima Guaman

Janelle Haack
Maureen Hafar
Calista Hagan
Deanna Hahn
Shari Hamann
Kristine Hanzelka
Jeanne Harris
Kylie Helm
Kimberly Heubner
Emily Hildebrand
Bridget Hill
Tanya Hoegh
Roberta Huff
Mary Hunzinger
Rachel Ingle
Amanda Johns
Debra Johnson
Rebecca Johnson
Gretchen Kealy
Jacqueline Keeling
Christina Kjar
Felisha Klouda
Heather Knight
Lois Knutson
Sarah Kowal
Lynne Krayer
Elizabeth Kreassig
Dana Lee
Hannah Leffler
Robin Linnevold
Kristen Lockerby
Susan Loftus
Rachel Lowry
Allyson Martin
Lisa Matthes

Heather McGlaughlin
Tara Meade
Michelle Meadows
Katherine Melloy
Sarah Menke
Heather Merrick
Jennifer Miller
Mara Miller
Bree Mills
Joelle Mixdorf
Krista Modracek
Melissa Mogan
Nicole Molumby
Katie Moore
Robyn Munkel
Ariela Myers
Nancy Nelson
Natalie Neshyba
Matthew Nipper
Daniel Perszyk
Elly Peterman
Alexandra Poppinga
Audrey Pritchett
Angela Reynolds
Lydia Richards
Jeanette Riepe
Gail Samuels
Kathleen Sander
Mary Schneider
Sara Shanley
Kerry Smith
Nanci Steman
Carissa Stout
Heather Thies
Stephanie Thimmesch

Rebekah Thompson
Jennifer Thompson
Mary Todey
Ryne Van Horn
Renee Veenstra
Daniel Velasco
Azeem Ward
Kristin Wells
Colleen Whitford
Sarah Wickett
Michael Will
Meredith Young

Oboe

Jill Anderson
Audrey Anderson
Annika Andrews
Terri Armfield
Elizabeth Boelk
Lisa Brende
Michele Burke
Julian Castillo
Karla Davis
Marina Elwood
Jo Anne Fosselman
David Frey
Michaella Garringer
Leslie Green
Claudio Rostrepo Guz-
man
Peter Hamlin
Brenna Herrmann
Aimee Higgins

Alicia Hopwood
William Jones
Sarah Karim
Mary Klemm
Kim Kochura
Stephanie Kruse
Grace Lau
Jeanette Loebach
Tonya Nagel
Christine Nebbia
Erin Nutting
Allison Offerman
Valerie Olson
Dane Philipsen
Aaron Reece
Jenifer Rieck
Sarah Ritchie
Stephanie Ruberg
Aryana Sarvestany
Lisa Schmitz
Janice Schwartz
Matthew Shipp
Laura Sindt
Nathan Smith
Kelly Stursma
Michelle Yoshimura
Cari Zuspann
Lucius Weathersby

Bassoon

Sarah Allen
Megan Austin
Jordan Bancroft-Smithe
Michael Bender
Carmen Borchardt
Barbara Breeding

Elizabeth Byerly
Joshua Carlo
Arielle Coffman
Markita Currie
Phillip Dann
Shelly Driscoll
Christine Fugate
Timothy Gale
Laurie Hoeppner
Linda Hulse
Joseph Keefe
Kristy King
Alan Kirkdorffer
Susan Kordick
Benjamin Lehnen
Florin Loghin
Sara Marolf
Bartley Meinke
Annalea Milligan
Charles Neff
Cassidy Olson
Katrina Phillips
Victoria Piper
Kathryn Pitts
Madeline Roach
Laura Sabato
Nancy Schlepp
David Schroeder
Devin Schroeder
Nolan Schroeder
Johanna Schumacher
Lisa Sehmann
Angela Staron
Clare Storkamp
Rachel Storm
Laurie Thomas
Benjamin Fox

Clarinet

Carol Achey
Kimberly Anderson
Erica Apple
Ashley Atkinson
Anne-Marie Bailey
Andrew Baker
Daniel Black
Michelle Boelman
Scott Bosco
Adrian Brown
Mary Brutsche
Jessica Buesing
Teresa Burkholder
Nicholas Carlo
Adam Clark
Kristi Cline
Hannah Coates
Elizabeth Cooney
Kendra Dahlstrom
Sarah Doty
Sarah Dowd
Laura Duvall
Arianna Edvenson
Elisha Eickholt
Megan Else
Renee Ferree
Molly Fewell
Rachel Fitkin
Julie Fletcher
Stacia Fortune
Therese Fosselman
Deborah Gaulrapp
Rose Gibson
Cynthia Gill
Sarah Gilpin
Elizabeth Glas

Warren Goodman
Timm Gould
Emily Goulson
Lori Graf
Hayley Graham
Rachel Gray
James Gummert
Jeffrey Guntren
Timothy Hackbart
Sheila Hadley
Lisa Hall
Aaron Hansen
Meghan Haw
Amy Hawley
Tianna Heien
Jillian Helscher
Lori Henning
Tami Huff
Michelle Hyde
Katy Johnson
Rachel Jones
Jeannette Kjos
John Kleinwolterink
Laura Knoll
Joseph Kreassig
Kristin Leaman
Shauna Lehmer
Amy Lentz
Carrie Long
Elizabeth Lynskey
Katlin MacBride
Lisa March
Jessica Martin
Cynthia Mason
Jennifer Mathison
Carol McBride
Ryan Middagh
Aviva Milner-Brage

Joni Mueller
Alisa Nagel
Jessica Nagle
Aimee Nielsen
Austin Nolan
Helen Northway
Kyle Novak
Corina O'Kones
Jocelyn Odergaard
Laura Olderog
Reece Oleson-King
Lori Olien
David Oline
Stephanie Opsal
Alissa Ortega
Laura Ortiz
Linda Overgaard
Lisa Overlie
Lisa Overman
Kathleen Owen
George Patti
Lucas Petersen
Emma Peterson
Olivia Randolph
Veronica Rasmussen
Ashley Richardson
Matthew Ridge
Shelley Ringgenberg
Laura Rodriguez
Theodore Roland
Alex Roth
Kelley Ryan
Elizabeth Schlotfeld
Emma Schmidt
Julie Schultz
Kimberly Schultz
Nicholas Schumacher
Amy Shipley

Julie Siebert
Abbey Silverman
Jill Sporer
Karen Stevens
Diane Strachan
Monica Streif
Christine Streight
Kariann Sullivan
Christine Todey
Nurhak Tuncer
Susan Ullrich
Nicole Vallentine
Carla Venteicher
Kristin Vierow
Michael Volz
Kendra Von Schaumburg
Shaara Wagner
Kelly Wells
Teresa Westphal
Rachel Wieckhorst
Andrew Wiele
Stephanie Williams
Elaine Wong
Austin Wright
Tonya Wurr
Lei Yang
Celeste Yeager
Madeline Young
Austin Zalatel
Glenn Zimmer

Saxophone

Gregory Aker
Eva Anderson
Scott Angelici
Karen Atkins

Randall Atkinson
Sarah Baker
Dustin Bear
William Beyer
Samuel Bills
Thomas Brown
Elizabeth Bunt
Ayodeji Coker
Lawrence Connell
Jessica Cronk
Jill Dempster
Clark Duhrkopf
April Fausch
Andrey Floryanovich
Lexi Forstrom
Jessica Gogerty
Katherine Haller
Wendy Hamann
Jason Henriksen
Andrew Hessenius
Randall Hoepker
Kevin Hoferer
Adam Hoffmann
Elke Hollingworth
Michael Hoover
Gregg Horas
Jeremy Jarvis
Katherine Johns
Trevor Jorgenson
Melissa Kacere
Joshua Lacher
Nick LeWarne
Jay Marcum
Marian Marturello
Jill McKim
Lane McMullen
Mason Meyers
Ryan Middleton

Brian Moore
Kyle Morgan
Michael Mullins
Todd Munnik
Jennifer Nebraska
Mark Northup
Paula O'Connell
David Oline
Teri Patrick
Jennifer Peters
Gregory Pittam
Rachel Price
David Primmer
Jay Ramsey
Rene Recinos
Keith Reynolds
Bryon Ruth
Jeffrey Schafer
Gabriel Scheid
Kamarie Schmidt
Gage Schmitt
Lisa Shankster
Traci Smith
Evan Smith
Thomas Sparks
Michelle Speich
Michael Stittsworth
Andrew Stolba
Richard Stone
Lisa Tackett
Tamara Thies
Teresa Thompson
Bradley Waline
Jane Welch
Jillian Whitaker
Scott Zimmer

Horn

Heidi Abrahamson
Jessica Anderson
Aaron Anderson
Gloria Becker
Katherine Berglof
Ruth Bradshaw
Anna Brandau
Erica Brizzi
Seth Butler
Benjamin Byersdorfer
Isaac Campbell
Ted Carpenter
Daniel Charette
Victoria Chargo
Casey Chlapek
Ashlyn Christensen
David Clark
Allison Clark
Mindy Coe
Kelly Coughlin
Heather Craighton
Catherine Crew
Wendy Crouse
Casey Dirksen
Leah Fank
Ann Fausch
Kathy Fowle
Roxanne Gaylord
Amanda Goepferich
Erin Guss
Nicolette Hagen
David Hall
Andrew Hamilton
Heather Hanawalt
Emily Hatch
Rebecca Helm

Mark Henderson
Wendy Hinman
Charlotte Hirsch
Katherine Holmer
Andrew van Hooreweghe
Laurie Johnson
Amber Johnson
Joshua Johnson
James Koning
Dylan Lanier
Melissa Lawson
Emily Linder
Brian Lovig
Valerie Lueders
Daniel Malloy
Francis Massinon
Ryan Miller
Brian Palmer
Patrick Parker
Jody Ploeger
Amanda Post
Cheryl Primmer
Meghan Reynolds
Sarah Robinson
Melissa Robinson
Tyler Ruberg
Anthony Schons
Brittany Schultz
Jackie Shannon
Christine Sherrod
Anne Slauson
Daniel Sniffin
Jacob Snyder
Forest Stewart
Leslie Twite
Laurie Van Der Pol
Meghan Walck
Mark Walters

Kyra Whitmore
Meridie Williams
Nicholas Wills
Jennifer Young

Trumpet

Leslie Aboud
Noah Alvarado
Drew Anderson
Christian Anderson
Christopher Arnold
Aaron Askam
Susan Bacher
Daniel Barth
Rachel Bearinger
Keth Benjamin
Bryan Bennett
Timothy Bennett
Brenna Blair
Jordan Boehm
Abigail Bogenrief
Chad Boydston
Lindsey Brunko
Gregory Bush
Anthony Butterworth
Marc Byers
John Carmichael
Kristi Chaplin
Kristi Colton
April Cook
Michael Drewes
Mark Duffy
Michael Erickson
Molly Evans
John Ferguson
Benjamin Feuerhelm

Kayla Fleming
Ryan Foizey
Mary Fosselman
Brett Fuller
Ryan Garmoe
Antonio Garza
Ann Gebel
Jon Godden
Meghan Guss
Allison Haag
Scott Hagarty
Faith Hall
Phillip Hamilton
Dianna Hinman
Maryann Hinman
Caroline Hlohowskyj
Toni Hoffman
Cooper Horning
Fred Hucke
Matthew Huddleston
Bradley Hurt
Tara Jueschke
Darren Junge
Wesley Keene
Steven Kenny
Jason Kirke
David Kjar
Daniel Kleinheinz
Rich Kolusu
Samuel Kreassig
David Krogan
Bret Lee
Laura Lefkow
Todd Lettow
Brandon Lewis
Eric Lins
Benjamin Logan
Paul Lubben

Chelsea Lusinski
Erin Maltby
Daniel Meier
Martin Menke
Ari Micich
Eric Miller
Michelle Most
Quentin Mussig
Emily Neuendorf
Christian Nietzschke
Margaret Nowacheck
David Oberhauser
John Oelrich
Glen Olson
Craig Parker
Branden Petersen
Matthew Peterson
Brandon Peterson
Joan Philgreen
Michael Prichard
Sarah Quesnell
Timothy Rall
David Rezek
Susan Rider
Vincente Rivera
Lance Schaefer
Melody Schilling
Dawn Schinckel
Leah Schmidt
Cory Schmitt
Brent Schultz
Brenda Sevcik
Caleb Shreves
Amber Smith
Bradley Stellmaker
Brooke Stevens
Nathan Stucky
Alex Thomas

Steven Tripolino
Christopher Van
Leeuwen
Logan Vander Weil
Paul Waech
Erin Wehr
Kelsey Wehr
Sara Woods
Corey Wright
Jerry Young
Daniel Zager

Trombone

John Alpers
Bryan Anton
Timothy Arnold
Paul Barnett
Roger Brown
Kevin Brown
Amy Cassill
Michael Conrad
Jonathan Coons
Zachary Cornell
Michael Cramer
Brian Crew
Nathan Currie
Jo Dee Davis
Philip Diderrich
Brian Dobbelaere
Levi Dressler
Abigail Feekes
Andrew Fletcher
Bridget Fosselman
Zachary Gignac
Kevin Hakes
Eleanor Henson

Carson Holloway
Paul Hovey
Jacob Humberg
Timothy Jones
Kyle Kennedy
Ronley King
Benjamin Klemme
Thomas Kling
Tabitha Langis
Paul Lichty
Matthew Lieberman
Jonathan Mallak
Brian Martin
Eileen Massinon
Lucy McBride
Theresa McDougal
Brent Mead
James Miller
Marte Murr
Joel Nagel
Paul Nielsen
Seth Nordin
Samuel Ogilvie
Mark Parsch
Adam Petersen
Myron Peterson
Joshua Piering
Andrew Pratt
Wade Presley
Paul Rappaport
Thomas Rauch
Michael Richardson
James Sanford
Sara Schmidt
Samuel Schmidt
Michael Schmitz
Nathan Spolar
Benjamin Stineman

Eric Stover
Michael Stow
Craig Sunken
Andrew Thoreen
Christopher Vanderpool
Nathan Vetter
Jeffrey Vogtlin
Christopher Walck
Spencer Walrath
Jon Wederquist
Nathaniel Welshons
Bradley Wheeler
Amy Wiemerslage
Anthony Williams
Jeffrey Young
James Young

Euphonium

David Adams
James Bohy
Alison Cook
Derek Danilson
John Day
Matthew Dutton
Michael Ellis
Elizabeth Frenchik
Lyle Hammond
Terra Hill
Paul Hochmuth
Anne Jackson
Charles Kelley
Jeffrey Kirkpatrick
Keith Koehlmoos
Joseph Kopacz
Samuel Nau
Karen Norby

Heather Noyes
Jill Pasterski
Kristin Pipho
Lydia Raim
Christopher Roling
Dean Saner
Mark Scheffer
Caryn Sowder
Chad Sowers
Brandon Toft
Steve Tunwall
Jeffrey Waldschmitt
Brandon Watson
Barbara Weiner
Justin Wells
Lyn Wickham
Elizabeth Witte
Angela Wrage
Kimiko Yamada

Tuba

Daniel Benson
Holly Botzum
Matthew Boucher
Keisetsu Chiba
Mark Cooper
Brett Copeland
Benjamin Creswell
Justin Davis
Adam Denner
Jeffrey Ensign
Katherine Gourley
Jacob Guellf
Walter Hicks
Taylor Hicks
Robert Hoffman

Aaron Hynds
Ryan Jonas
Michael Jones
Nathan Jones
Brian Kiser
Timothy Kramer
James Livingston
Christofer Lockwood
Scott Lueders
Andrew Mattison
Nicholas Menke
Alan Moore
Kyosuke Nakata
Heather Noyes
Loras Schissel
Gregory Simmons
Kevin Taylor
Kevin Teno
Ryan Thomas
Casey Turner
Marcus Wigim
Sung Joo Yoo
Trevis Young
John Zauche

Contrabass

Robert Bill
Andrew Braught
Brittny Gish
Matthew Glascock
Tyler Huckfelt
Cara Keller
Eric Krieger
Nathan Lienhard
Richard Meide
Joseph Mnayer

Patrick Murphy
Brian Robison
Mark Scheffer
Christopher Schwartz
Brian Scoggins
Daniel Shook
Mark Sonksen
Dmitri Vasilov
Kyle Whalley
Craig Woelber

Piano

Jessica Anderson
Isaac Brockshus
Seth Butler
Debra Hoepker
Elisabed Imerlishvili
Ja-Hyeong Koo
Kaitlin McCrary
James Mick
Edwin Neimann
Jessica Schick
Chad Schmertmann

Harp

Ali Bissell
Denise Brewster
Jennifer Kinley
Mardi Mahaffey
Janet Peterson
Megan Schuh
Acacia Scott
Suzanne Sontag
Jennifer Souder

Jacquelyn Venter
Renee Wilson

Percussion

Cathy Anderson
Matthew Andreini
Lori Atkinson
Nicholas Bailey
Bryan Bales
Kimberly Bata
Justin Baumgartner
Nicholas Behrends
Nathaniel Benzing
Marcus Bishop
Michael Bockholt
Kyler Boss
Todd Boyd
Megan Brasch
Grant Burns
Lisa Busch
Thomas Capps
Brett Clark
Kristin Conrad
Benjamin Cook-Feltz
Brian Cooper
Stephen Crawford
Patrick Cunningham
Jacob Davis
Ryan DeCook
Brian Dellinger
Ivan Doutt
Barry Dvorak
Garrett Dwyer
Trevor Else
Brannon Fells
Joseph Finnegan

Nicholas Flores
Ryan Frost
Ryan Greiner
Jeffry Griffin
Darin Haack
Katie Hammond
Christopher Hansen
Eric Hanson
Nathaniel Hawkins
Linda Heacock
Joshua Hearn
Bradley Heddinger
Ryan Hoagland
Steven Hoopingarner
Matthew Hoskins
Barbara Hoth
Bradley Hurd
Bradley Jacobson

Jack Jean
Christopher Jensen
Tyler Kalina
Barbara Kriegh
David Kuehn
Cindy Lack
Alex Lafrenz
Nicholas Lake
Nicholas LeGuillou
Phillip Martin
Kody McKracken
Thomas Myers
David Nanke
James Nielsen
Gregory Nordmeyer
Connie O'Meara
Dennis O'Neill
Aaron Ottmar

Brenda Peel
Sean Phelan
David Posz
Randy Ramaekers
Joseph Rebik
Mathias J. Ribyn
Marie Rice
Elina Riley
Eric Schmitz
Valerie Schnekloth
Michael Schumacher
Andrew Seiffert
Jason Senchina
Steven Shanley
Samantha Skaalen
Jeffrey Smith
Teresa Smith
Sal Sofia

Stephen Sporer
Randall Stahl
Delayne Stallman
Adrian Suarez
Michael Thursby
David Tiede
Brett Umthun
Charles Van Haecke
Richard Wagoner
Christopher Ward
Marilyn Weaverling
Benjamin Wells
Jane Whitehead
Ashley Williams
Kathrine Wilson
Elizabeth Zihlman

Guest Artists

IT WAS MY INTENTION to have a guest artist, or chorus, perform
with us each season. There are sixty-nine soloists, quintets, quartets, and choruses indicated as our guests. There were several who
performed several times with us, so we averaged about three guests
for each season. These would include the winners of the Wind
Symphony Solo Competition, open to any wind player in the School
of Music. In the early years of the Northern Festival of Bands, we
also extended an invitation to the winner of that event's Solo Competition. But, within a few years, we dropped that as it proved to
be quite cumbersome in scheduling. The School of Music enjoyed
an excellent Artist Faculty, and I tried to have at least one of them
perform with us each year. And, because of my desire to perform
large choral works, we tried to include one or more of our choral
ensembles every few years.

Bert Aalders (Netherlands)	Conductor
Elizabeth Anderson	Violin
Matthew Andreini	Percussion
Thomas Barry	Oboe, Saxophone
Harry Begian	Conductor
Cayla Bellamy	Bassoon
Keith Benjamin	Trumpet
Jeffrey Brich	Tenor
Christopher Buckholz	Trombone
Rebecca Burkhardt	Conductor
Hunter Capoccioni	Contrabass
David Clark	Horn
Steven Colton	Conductor
Jo Dee Davis	Trombone
Lorenzo Della Fonte (Italy)	Conductor
Angeleita Floyd	Flute
Jeffrey Funderburk	Tuba
Robin Galloway	Trumpet
Randy Grabowski	Trumpet
Jack Graham	Clarinet

Robin Guy	Piano
Frederick Halgedahl	Violin
Kevin Hanna	Trombone
Jon Hansen	Trombone
Felix Hauswirth (Switzerland)	Conductor
John Hines	Bass
Randy Hogancamp	Timpani
Morgan Horning	Soprano
Matthew Huddleston	Trumpet
William Johnson	Conductor
Fritz Kaenzig	Tuba
John Kleinwolterink	Clarinet
András Körtesi (Hungary)	Piano
Leia Lensing	Mezzo Soprano
John Locke	Conductor
Daniel Malloy	Horn
László Marosi (Hungary)	Conductor
Amanda McCandless	Clarinet
Jean McDonald	Soprano
Ryan Middleton	Saxophone
Luke Miller	Tuba
Leslie Morgan	Soprano
John Mueller	Euphonium
Steven Mumford	Horn
Glen Olson	Trumpet
Jesse Orth	Tuba
Aaron Ottmar	Percussion
Heather Peyton	Oboe
Jody Ploeger	Horn
Raif Primo (Israel)	Conductor
Janis Purins (Latvia)	Conductor
Claudio Re (Italy)	Conductor
Denis Salvini (Italy)	Conductor
Michael Schuler (Switzerland)	Conductor
Nicholas Schumacher	Clarinet
William Shepherd	Conductor
Daniel Sniffin	Horn
Louis Stout	Horn

Kariann Sullivan	Clarinet
Thomas Tritle	Horn, piano
Raymond Tymas-Jones	Tenor
Robert Washut	Piano
David Whitwell	Conductor
Nicholas Wills	Horn
Northern Brass Quintet	Brass Quintet
UNI Varsity Men's Glee Club	Chorus
UNI Concert Chorale	Chorus
UNI Women's Chorus	Chorus
UNI Singers	Chorus

Audio Recordings

RAINBOW GARDENS (1990) (audio cassette)

Amilcare Ponchielli	Italy, 1834–1886	*Gran Marcia, "Milano"* (c. 1860)
Percy Aldridge Grainger	Australia/USA, 1882–1961	*Country Gardens* (c.1918)
		Lads of Wamphrey (1904)
Aram Khatchaturian	Armenia, 1903–1978	*Armenian Folk Songs* (1932)
David Bedford	England, 1937–2011	*Sun Paints Rainbows on the Vast Waves* (1982)
Karel Husa	Czech/USA, 1921–2016	*Smetana Fanfare* (1982)
Jerome Sorcsek	USA, b. 1949	*Portrait of Faustus* (1978)
Ron Nelson	USA, b. 1929	*Medieval Suite* (1983)

MEMORIES (1994)

Carl Orff/J. Krance	Germany, 1895–1982	*Carmina Burana* (1936)
Frigyes Hidas	Hungary, 1928–2007	*Circus Suite* (1985)
Hans Werner Henze	Germany, 1926–2012	*Ragtimes and Habaneras* (1975)
Zdenek Lukás	Czech, 1928–2007	*Musica Boema* (1977)

GENESIS (1995)

Jean Balissat	Switzerland, 1936–2007	*La Premier Jour* (1993)
Ralph Hultgren	Australia, b. 1953	*Symphony for Wind Orchestra* (1994)
Charles Cushing	USA, 1905–1982	*Angel Camp* (1952)
Zdenek Jonák	Czech, 1917–1995	*Ciacona in e-moll* (1993)

REQUIEM (1997)

Nikolai Rimsky-Korsakov	Russia, 1844–1908	*Cortege aus "Mlada"* (1892)
György Ránki	Hungary, 1907–1993	*Suite from Pomádé Király Uj Ruhája* (1954)
Daniel Bukvich	USA, b. 1954	*Meditations on the Writings of Vasily Kandinsky* (1996)
		Jeffrey Funderburk, tuba
David Whitwell	USA, b. 1937	*Sinfonia da Requiem ... in memory of Mozart* (1988)

THE BEST OF ALL POSSIBLE WORLDS (2004)

Dana Wilson	USA, b. 1946	*Shortcut Home* (2000)
Percy Aldridge Grainger	Australia/USA, 1882–1961	*Country Gardens* (1919)
		Colonial Song (1918)
		Molly on the Shore (1920)
Charles Ives/R. Thurston	USA, 1874–1954	*The Alcotts* (1947)
John Williams/P. Lavender	USA, b. 1932	*1941* (1979)
Eric Whitacre	USA, b. 1970	*October* (2000)
Leonard Bernstein	USA, 1918–1990	*Suite from Candide* (1956)
Robert Rumbelow	USA, b. 1965	*Night* (2002)

Wind Symphony Video Productions

Henk Badings (Netherlands, 1907–1987)
Armageddon (1968)
November 20, 2014
https://youtu.be/C90v8vvF0qI

James Beckel (USA, b. 1948)
The Glass Bead Game (1997)
October 4, 2013
https://youtu.be/uWuoN4JEntY

Leonard Bernstein (USA, 1918–1990)
Suite from Candide (1956)
October 5, 2016
https://youtu.be/bS2sZ2tMVyA

Daniel Bukvich (USA, b. 1954)
Symphonic Movement (2016)
April 24, 2017
https://youtu.be/8n08WDbyfVY

Daniel Bukvich (USA, b. 1954)
Meditations on the Writings of Vasily Kandinsky (1996)
https://youtu.be/etMs-tu3d84

Nathan Daughtrey (USA, b. 1975)
Concerto for Vibraphone (2012)
November 20, 2015
https://youtu.be/3-j9D8Wi06M

Jacob DeHaan (Netherlands, b. 1959)
Nerval's Poems (2007)
April 18, 2016
https://youtu.be/hC-IDKXBDqs

Timo Forsström (Finland, b. 1961)
Sons of the Midnight Sun (2012)
April 24, 2017
https://youtu.be/2hT0B0TfOcI

Frigyes Hidas (Hungary, 1928–2007)
Vidám Zene (Merry Music) (1983)
November 20, 2014
https://youtu.be/keRuYWKg7Pc

Frigyes Hidas (Hungary, 1928–2007)
Double Concerto (2001)
April 18, 2016
https://youtu.be/DGWfBLCYFRA

Karel Husa (Czech/USA, 1921–2016)
Music for Prague, 1968 (1968)
April 3, 2013
https://youtu.be/kp9K2JphLmI

Karel Husa (Czech/USA, 1921–2016)
Apotheosis of This Earth (1970)
November 18, 2016
Movt 1: https://youtu.be/hTLf4REaIGg
Movt 2: https://youtu.be/9zjYRYP-9Qc
Movt 3: https://youtu.be/CEWahSTslEQ

Karel Husa (Czech/USA, 1921–2016)
Smetana Fanfare (1984)
April 3, 2013
https://youtu.be/Mwm2ZFyXhSs

Guillermo Lago (Netherlands, b. 1960)
Cuidades: Sarajevo (Bosnia and Herzegovina) (2011)
November 18, 2016
https://youtu.be/Pla_v4046Yg

Zdenek Lukás (Czech Republic, 1928–2007)
Musica Boema (1976)
April 3, 2013
`https://youtu.be/iJX5Asu-tlE`

David Maslanka (USA, 1953–2017)
Short Symphony: Give Us This Day (2007)
April 18, 2016
`https://youtu.be/ZOh4AM82k4E`

David Maslanka (USA, 1953–2017)
Requiem (2013)
November 18, 2016
`https://youtu.be/pTUbNE0BChM`

Hardy Mertens (Netherlands, b. 1960)
The Butterfly Lovers (2008)
April 18, 2016
`https://youtu.be/Hq1iJrQX7Mc`

Hardy Mertens (Netherlands, b. 1960)
Xenia Sarda (1996)
October 4, 2013
`https://youtu.be/DXggbnAh2Nw`

Vacláv Nelhybel (Czech Republic, 1919–1996)
Symphonic Movement (1966)
November 20, 2014
`https://youtu.be/1H_3IN0sTzg`

Vaclav Nelhybel (Czech/USA, 1919-1996)
Trittico (1963)
April 3, 2013
`https://youtu.be/6uUWA3aN_BA`

Rolf Rudin (Germany, b. 1961)
Requiem, op 70 (2005)
April 17, 2015
I. Introitus: `https://youtu.be/SmZ5VQqEcXc`
II. Kyrie: `https://youtu.be/3YLZB3L81N0`
III. Graduale: `https://youtu.be/Csm4ULyS_RU`
IV. Pie Jesu: `https://youtu.be/lGJp5Eiealg`
V. Sanctus: `https://youtu.be/fxkVwh9D6jA`
VI. Agnus Dei: `https://youtu.be/6SpLISsJepk`
VII. Communio - Lux Aeterna: `https://youtu.be/PfsdQjTvCaQ`
VIII. Responsorium - Libera Me: `https://youtu.be/GdMtFctRPIM`
IX. In Paradisum: `https://youtu.be/Hyz8jbZeZw4`

Rolf Rudin (Germany, b. 1961)
Te Deum, op 93 (2017)
April 24, 2017
`https://youtu.be/vRc4mfrOD5g`

Ivan Trevino (USA, b. 1983)
Strive to be Happy
October 5, 2016
`https://youtu.be/ePVT4gqe_Qk`

Robert Washut (USA, b. 1951)
The High Road (2013)
April 18, 2016
`https://youtu.be/CTyD8RmKu4M`

Jillian Whitaker (USA, b. 1992)
Coming Home (2016)
April 24, 2017
`https://youtu.be/BD4jdGeIBvM`

Satoshi Yagisawa (Japan, b. 1975)
Hymn to the Sun With the Beat of Mother Earth (2005)
November 18, 2016
https://youtu.be/RGh68o7dUaA

Northern Iowa Wind Symphony with Varsity Men's
Glee Club
November 15, 2013
Richard Burchard, *Creator alme siderum*
Ron Nelson, *Homage to Leonin*
Franz Biebl, *Ave Maria*
Frank Ticheli, *Angels in the Architecture*
David Whitwell, *Sinfonia da Requiem*
Performed in memoriam on the occasion of the 50th
anniversary of the death of President John Fitzgerald
Kennedy (May 29, 1917 – November 22, 1963)
https://youtu.be/7wjjRw4_RcA

Bravi: Wind Symphony Tour in Italy 2012
https://youtu.be/-uICOawh-YI

Wind Symphony in Bergamo, Italy 2012
https://youtu.be/PKOA4TL7TSQ

Italia 2012: A Photo Montage
https://youtu.be/j62TJbC9MaI

Italia 2016: A Photo Montage
https://youtu.be/C-13aYeHY5g

Northern Iowa Wind Symphony 1982–2017 (Photo
Montage)
https://youtu.be/QV26QnVDkao

The Wind Symphony: Final Concert (Photo Montage)
https://youtu.be/aud3EpzWFG4

Index

About the Author

RONALD JOHNSON is Director of Bands Emeritus, and Professor Emeritus of Music at the University of Northern Iowa. He was a member of the faculty in the School of Music, conducting the Wind Symphony and the Chamber Wind Players, from the fall of 1982 until his retirement in the spring of 2017. His formal education includes degrees from Texas Tech University (1968), California State University, Northridge (1971), and the University of Illinois (1985), and his teachers include David Whitwell, Mircea Cristescu (Romania), and Harry Begian. Prior to his appointment at Northern Iowa, he was Conductor of the Wind Symphony at Modesto Junior College (CA) from 1972 until 1979, where he developed one of the most distinguished two-year programs in the nation.

Dr. Johnson has appeared as a guest artist, both as conductor and teacher, with professional and municipal ensembles in China, Germany, Hong Kong, Hungary, Israel, Italy, Latvia, Slovenia, Spain, Sweden, and Switzerland. In the 2004–2005 academic year, he received a Fulbright Senior Lecturer Award, under the auspices of the U.S. Department of State. For that year, Dr. Johnson served as a member of the Music Faculty at the Pécsi Tudományegyetem (University of Pécs) in Hungary, where he created and conducted the Harmónia, a small wind group specializing in original wind music of the 18th and 19th centuries. In 2002, in a ceremony in Vatican City (Rome), for "significant contributions to humanity," he was invested in L' Ordre des Chevaliers du Sinai (The Religious and Military Order of the Knights of St. Catherine of Sinai).

During his tenure at Northern Iowa, the Wind Symphony took six European Concert Tours ... three in Hungary, and three in Italy. One can find some 33 Wind Symphony videos posted on YouTube. The ensemble produced five audio recordings: *Rainbow Gardens* (1990) (audio cassette), *Memories* (1994), *Genesis* (1995), *Requiem* (1997), and *the best of all possible worlds* (2004).

Dr. Johnson has been given the Silver Baton Award by Kappa Kappa Psi Band Fraternity; the Orpheus Award from Phi Mu Alpha Music Fraternity, and an honorary diploma from Il Conservatorio Luca Marenzio di Brescia in Italy.